TWAYNE'S WORLD AUTHORS SERIES

A Survey of the World's Literature

SPAIN

Janet W. Díaz, University of North
Carolina at Chapel Hill

EDITOR

Miguel Hernández

TWAS 464

Miguel Hernández
A sketch from life by Antonio Buero Vallejo

MIGUEL HERNÁNDEZ

By GERALDINE CLEARY NICHOLS

Colgate University

TWAYNE PUBLISHERS

A DIVISION OF G. K. HALL & CO., BOSTON

Library of Congress Cataloging in Publication Data

Nichols, Geraldine Cleary.
  Miguel Hernández.

  (Twayne's World Authors Series; TWAS 464 : Spain)
  Bibliography: p. 191–96
  Includes index.
  1. Hernández, Miguel, 1910–1942—Criticism and inter-
pretation.
PQ6615.E57Z86   861'.6'2   77-19102
ISBN 0-8057-6301-5

To my mother
Mary Louise O'Haire
And to the memory of my grandmother
Mary Charlotte Ryan

Contents

About the Author

Geraldine Cleary Nichols graduated *magna cum laude* with Distinction in Spanish from Duke University in 1967. Awarded a Woodrow Wilson Fellowship for 1968, she received her M.A. and Ph.D. degrees from the Johns Hopkins University. She is presently Assistant Professor of Spanish at Colgate University. Other publications include an article in *Journal of Spanish Studies: Twentieth Century* 3, No. 3, "Dialectical Realism and Beyond: *Últimas tardes con Teresa*," and another in the *Journal of Hispanic Philology* 1, No. 3, entitled "The Rehabilitation of the Duke of Ferrara."

Preface

The twentieth-century poet Miguel Hernández occupies an important but ill-defined place in the history of Spanish poetry. Important not only because his lyrics are among the finest and most original which have been written in Spain, but also because he influenced many of the major poets of the postwar years; ill-defined because in a poetically rich century easily divided into generations or schools—Modernism, the Generations of 1927 and 1936, the First and Second Postwar Generations, etc.—Miguel Hernández stands alone. Coming of poetic age just after the brilliant Generation of 1927, sharing only some of the characteristics of the disputed Generation of 1936[1]—and dead before that group really established itself—Hernández defies easy classification. The vertiginous personal and poetic changes which he underwent in the twelve short years of his maturity complicate the task of evaluation even further.

It is in part this anomalous quality, coupled with his intensely dramatic life, which have led most critics to approach Hernández biographically. Then, too, his poetry is "essentially direct confession and witness of things, intensely interwoven with the emotional and civil vicissitudes of the man," as Dario Puccini points out, so that it "requires, precisely, an investigation that is sympathetic to and always invigorated by his biography."[2] Admittedly, Hernández's work is transparently confessional, and one cannot fully appreciate such work without knowing something of its biographical antecedents.[3] Yet while I shall give considerable attention to biography, the primary focus of this study will be Hernández's work. I shall trace the trajectory of this work, following its evolution through the twelve years of his mature production, analyzing both its elements of continuity and its changes.

From his earliest attempts at verse in the Golden Age manner or his Calderonian miracle play, through his cryptic *Songs and Ballads of Absence*, to the desolate "Last Poems," Hernández pondered the basic themes of sex, love, death, and self-perpetuation. His work, externally characterized by a succession of styles and genres, by radical changes in diction and tropology, nonetheless manifests an underlying continuity, both in theme and in the archetypal symbols which he used to represent various aspects of those themes. Studied closely, the changes in style and orientation resolve themselves into three well-defined periods which I have labeled Youth (1930–36), the War Years (1936–39), and the Last Years (1939–41.)[4]

Hernández's influence on contemporary or younger poets is difficult to assess for several reasons. Principal among these is the fact that his work was so severely censored by the Franco government (against which Hernández had fought during the Civil War and in whose prisons he died) that we cannot presume most of the young poets were able to read it in its entirety.

Hernández has been likened to García Lorca in that both died at the hands of the Nationalists in Spain's Civil War: Lorca at thirty-six, in the early days of the war, Hernández at thirty-two, on the third anniversary of the war's formal end. Both have been somewhat mythified as a result, yet neither Lorca nor Hernández needs such spurious fame: Lorca has been established as one of the best poets in the history of Spanish letters; Hernández will one day stand beside him.

In translating Hernández's poetry I have made no attempt to reproduce its rhythm or sounds. I have preferred to give as literal a translation as possible, my only care being that the words flow rather well in English, and that they reproduce insofar as possible the flavor or tone (i.e., abstruse, vulgar, disruptive) of the words in Spanish. All translations of the prose (Hernández's or his critics') are also mine.

I gratefully acknowledge the permission of Hernández's widow Josefina Manresa to quote from her husband's works. I am also indebted to the Colgate Research Council for a grant which financed the research for this book.

GERALDINE CLEARY NICHOLS

Colgate University

Chronology

1910   October 30: Miguel Hernández is born in Orihuela (Alicante) to Concepción Gilabert Giner and Miguel Hernández Sánchez.

1918   Enrolled in school.

1925   Leaves school to help father with herds.

1930   Publishes his first poems in local newspapers. Friendship with Ramón Sijé.

1931– (December–May): First trip to Madrid; his poetry is ignored
1932   and he is unable to find work. Returns to Orihuela; begins to write in the Neo-Gongorine style.

1933   Publishes *Perito en lunas (Expert in Moons)*.

1934   Falls in love with Josefina Manresa, his future wife. Second trip to Madrid, armed with his *auto sacramental* (miracle play) *Quien te ha visto y quien te ve y Sombra de lo que eras (How You've Changed! and A Shadow of Your Former Self)*; play's publication in *Cruz y Raya* brings him the favorable attention of the highest literary circles. Enters a period of spiritual crisis characterized by political and religious doubts.

1935   Continues in Madrid, becoming especially close to vanguard poets Aleixandre and Neruda. Completes *El rayo que no cesa (The Unending Thunderbolt)* and the play *Los hijos de la piedra (Sons of Stone)*. Sijé dies.

1936   *The Unending Thunderbolt,* including an elegy to Sijé, is published and acclaimed. Abandons the sonnet for the freer forms of Aleixandre and Neruda. Works on the play *El labrador de más aire (The Comeliest Peasant)*. War begins. Six weeks later he enlists in the Republican Army.

1937   Marries Josefina in a civil ceremony. Publishes *The Comeliest Peasant, Viento del pueblo (Wind of the People)* and *Teatro en la guerra (Wartime Theater)*. Travels to Russia, representing the Republic at the Fifth Festival of the Theater in Moscow (August). Son Manuel Ramón is born while Miguel is at the front in Teruel.

1938   Publishes *El pastor de la muerte (The Shepherd of Death)*. Continues to travel all over Spain. Health poor. Manuel

Ramón dies at ten months. Miguel suffers an emotional breakdown.

1939 Son Manuel Miguel is born. *El hombre acecha (Man the Spy)* is printed but never bound. The war ends (March). Miguel crosses into Portugal; is returned to Spanish authorities by the Portuguese. Tortured and imprisoned. Released from prison (September). Returns home, bringing with him most of the poetry for the *Cancionero y romancero de ausencias (Songs and Ballads of Absence)*. Reapprehended, reimprisoned.

1940 Condemned to death; sentence commuted to thirty years imprisonment. Moved from prison to prison. Campaigns to be transferred nearer Josefina.

1941 Transferred to Alicante. Contracts tuberculosis complicated by paratyphoid fever. Little food, no medicine.

1942 March 28, third anniversary of war's end. Miguel dies.

1952 Publication of his *Obra escogida (Selected Works)* in Spain.

1960 Publication of his *Obras completas (Complete Works)* in Buenos Aires.

1976 Publication of his *Obra poética completa (Complete Poetic Works)* in Spain.

CHAPTER 1

The Trajectory of Hernández's Work

BEFORE beginning a more detailed analysis of the three phases of Hernández's work, it is well to outline briefly the constants and the changes within those phases. The most evident changes in his work are structural: style, form, syntax, vocabulary, genres. There are also marked changes in subject matter and, to a lesser extent, in the choice of themes. On the basis of these changes we can divide his work heuristically into the aforementioned three periods. With the exception of the play *Sons of Stone* (1935) and of a dozen or so poems written during an experimental six-month period immediately before the outbreak of the Civil War, these divisions are remarkably clear-cut.

The elements which persist through Hernández's work are a number of natural symbols: moon, shadow, light, sun, water, rock, earth, dust, rivers, blood, and wind; and certain great universal concerns of man: sex, death, love, and the hope of eternal return. During the successive periods in his writing the continuing symbols take on different shades of meaning,[1] and different aspects of the major concerns or themes emerge. His attitude toward love, sex, or death (and the symbols he used in writing about them), for example, changed markedly from his adolescence to the years before his death. But the themes themselves are constants. With the sexual theme, we see that at first sex is equated with an overpowering lust; then it becomes part of a conjugal, romantic love; and finally a means for the couple to fulfill and perpetuate themselves. The theme of death is first regarded with a melancholy concern (usually identified by Hernández scholars as his "tragic fatalism"),[2] then with defiance, and in the last period, first with fear and a desire to thwart it, then with acceptance. Love is first focused on himself and on women, then on his comrades-in-arms, then on his family, and finally, on all mankind.[3] Hernández's hope for immortality or eternal return was persistent. In his first period, the hope centered on an agricultural sort of rebirth; in the second, on immortality won by fighting or writing for the Republic; in the third, on his son. Thus while these four concerns remained vital to Hernández throughout his life, his feelings about them changed and evolved, so that even within the continuous we find change.

Looking again at the "natural" symbols and "universal" themes which characterize Hernández's work, it is evident that all are archetypal. Briefly let us define what we mean by "archetypal"—a word which has been used so loosely as to have become imprecise[4]—because it provides an invaluable critical tool for the study of Hernández's work. Essentially we shall follow C. G. Jung's definition of the archetype: "forms or images of a collective nature which occur practically all over the earth as constituents of myths and at the same time as autochthonous products of unconscious origin."[5] Mircea Eliade simplifies that definition, describing archetypes as "those great symbols which the soul finds immediately expressive."[6] One of Jung's disciples, Erich Neumann, has elaborated and made more systematic Jung's theory of the archetype, showing how man passes under the influence of various archetypes during his development: "the individual ego consciousness has to pass through the same archetypal stages which determined the evolution of consciousness in the life of humanity . . . . Ego consciousness evolves by passing through a series of 'eternal images,' and the ego, transformed in the passage, is constantly experiencing a new relation to the archetypes."[7] Much as mankind, passing through the series of archetypes, left traces of its journey in a sequence of mythological images, the creative individual, maturing and passing under the influence of successive archetypes, will leave traces of his development in the successive myths and symbol clusters which appear in his work.[8] Such is the case with Miguel Hernández; the successive changes which even the "constants" or archetypal elements in his work undergo find an explanation in Neumann's hypothesis.

The three periods into which Hernández's work divides itself correspond to the three major archetypes which dominate all developing egos (I follow Neumann's *Origins* here). In the first period of life the dominant archetype is that of the Creation Myth. The ego is still nascent, "contained in the unconscious," unable to differentiate itself from the "Great Mother." For a time the dependent being enjoys this state, glorying in the Mother's munificence. In Hernández's poetry corresponding to this stage we see him delighting in the fertile Levantine landscape, describing it so frequently that numerous critics say the "Levantine character" of his verse is one of its distinguishing traits.

Eventually, the embryonic consciousness begins to seek independence, struggling to break the hold of the unconscious, or Great Mother, which is now perceived as being malevolent. In Hernández's work of this period, we see him fighting strongly against the pull of the "unconscious," identified almost exclusively in his mind with the libido. For Hernández this is a religious period: he looks to God (archetypally known as the Spirit Father) to save him from the call of the chthonic. In the agonized love poetry of *The Unending Thunderbolt* we see the final stage of his struggle to resist the pull of the Feminine. He knows he can be annihilated by this passion.

Miguel's second period reflects the archetype of the Hero, who, fortified in his masculinity (or consciousness) by cadres of other young men, is now strong enough to attack the Mother, in the hope of establishing a new order on earth. For Hernández, the fight was against the old order in Spain, represented by the Nationalists, whom he continually described as feminine.

In the third period, the last years, Hernández's work shows him to be under the influence of the Transformation Archetype. The Hero establishes a patriarchy, cultivates the inner virtues, and finally becomes centroverted (psychologically self-sufficient), facing death with equanimity. Hernández died so young that I suspect he never fully lived out this final archetype. Certainly we find little evidence in his last poems that he felt his life had come full circle, but perhaps the virtual silence of his last eighteen months was an expression of his acceptance of death.

The archetypal approach, one of several we will employ in studying Hernández's evolution, provides important insights into his choice of symbols and themes, as well as into the changes they underwent as he matured. Since one of the major objectives of this study is to chart the diachronic pattern of Hernández's work, the importance of this sort of criticism should be readily apparent.

CHAPTER 2

Youth and Early Manhood (1926–36)

I Biography and Intellectual Formation

MIGUEL Hernández was born on October 30, 1910, to poor parents in the village of Orihuela in the sunny, fertile Mediterranean province of Alicante. His father, Miguel Hernández Sánchez, was a herdsman dealing in goats and sheep. From the beginning he opposed, as any uneducated peasant might, his son's literary endeavors.[1] Miguel's mother, Concepción Gilabert Giner, was a quiet and resigned woman, prematurely aged, who always tried to temper her husband's rages against the children.

The extent of Miguel's formal schooling has been disputed, with most critics believing that he attended school for only two or three years. However, María de Gracia Ifach's recent biography presents convincing evidence that in fact Hernández's schooling lasted for seven years, from 1918 to 1925 (pp. 18–23). After her revelation, the legend of Miguel's superhuman autodidacticism may be laid to rest. He began school in an annex of the famous Jesuit Colegio de Santo Domingo. The annex, staffed by lay teachers, was for the poor children of Orihuela. Miguel's intelligence was quickly recognized, and he was invited to attend the Colegio itself. He continued to excel, so that the Jesuits soon tried—unsuccessfully—to convince the boy's father to allow him to continue his studies through the university level at their expense. According to Vicente, his father mulishly refused because he needed the young Miguel to help with the herds, and he did not think it just that one son be a professional while the other was a goatherd. At the age of fifteen, then, Miguel left the Colegio to tend his father's goats. His formal education was over, but a long and fruitful period of literary autodidacticism had begun.

Miguel borrowed books haphazardly all over Orihuela. "The first things I read were the novels of Luis de Val and of Pérez Escrich" (two prolific Levantine authors best known for their serialized novels), he related in an interview during his first visit to Madrid in 1932 (quoted in Zardoya, *Miguel Hernández*, p. 10). With some guidance from Don Luis Almarcha, canon of the Cathedral of Orihuela (and later from Ramón Sijé), his readings took a more classical direction: Cervantes, Lope de Vega, Góngora and Garcilaso, San Juan de la Cruz (St. John of the Cross), and Virgil (in Fray Luis de León's translation). Almarcha wrote: "I have never had another disciple who was so profoundly impressed with Virgil and St. John of the Cross" (Cano Ballesta, p. 330). Among the modern poets he read were Jorge Guillén, Antonio Machado, Juan Ramón Jiménez (his favorite), Gabriel y Galán, Rubén Darío, Valéry and Verlaine (almost certainly in translation); and in prose, a fellow Levantine, Gabriel Miró, whom he identified as his favorite writer, and the one who had probably influenced him most.[2]

Above all, the young man's singleness of mind stands out. He read incessantly, so absorbed that he occasionally lost track of his herd. He read late into the night, disobeying his father and suffering from the man's violent rages whenever he was caught. Very conscious of the family's low social class and its poverty, and of his own poor education, Miguel seemed driven to better himself. Against all odds, "his dream was to study and to write," his wife remembers (Zardoya, *Miguel Hernández*, p. 12). An early poem begins: "En cuclillas ordeño / una cabrita y un sueño" ("Crouching, I milk / A goat and a dream," cited in Ifach, p. 17).

He began to write when he was sixteen: prose poems, poetry, and possibly some dramatic scenes. He continued to read and write in relative isolation until he was eighteen, when he began to meet with a group of young would-be authors like himself: Carlos and Efrén Fenoll, Ramón and Gabriel Sijé (pen names for José and Justino Marín Gutiérrez). In the back room of the Fenolls' bakery they discussed literary topics, read their own works, and planned the cultural regeneration of Orihuela.

The association with Ramón Sijé was to be decisive in Hernández's intellectual development. Two years younger than Miguel, Sijé was precociously brilliant; widely read; a promising literary scholar (although he was attending law school); and a militant, reform-minded Catholic. Orihuela, immortalized by Gabriel Miró as "Oleza" in *Nuestro Padre San Daniel* and in *El Obispo leproso*, was renowned for its archconservative, even fanatical, Catholicism, in many cases purely external. The publication in 1926 of *El Obispo leproso* "shook the somnolent Orihuelan atmosphere" (Ramos, p. 25), and divided the intellectuals of the community into two camps: those in favor of maintaining the Oleza Miró had described, and those who wished to change it. In spite of his youth, Sijé became one of the leading figures in the latter group. Through various cultural / recreational associations, in numerous articles, and finally in two short-lived magazines which he helped to found—*Voluntad* (March–July 1930) and *El Gallo Crisis* (four issues, June 1934– Spring 1935)—, Sijé advocated a regeneration of Spain through the return to a more intimate "Catholicism of the home, not of the plaza."[3] He believed that literature—especially dramatic literature, as in the Golden Age—was the ideal medium for converting the common people to his ideals. Fittingly, he judged the style of the Baroque or Counter Reformation, which was eminently religious, to be "the eternal form of culture."[4]

Puccini (pp. 32–35) judges the value of Sijé's influence to have been both negative and positive. It was negative because it led Miguel inevitably toward two deleterious extremes, the abstract conceptist lyricism of *Expert in Moons* or the "sermon resolved into lyrical forms," *How You've Changed!* Yet "on a strictly formal level, it had two undeniable merits": it forced Miguel to put his poetry through a "complex exercise, first mimetic (metaphorical), then conceptual (allegorical), before recovering it, laden with meanings (thus his semantic extremism) and symbols (thus his parabolic extremism)"; and secondly, it forced him into serious reading of the mystical and Baroque poets of the sixteenth and seventeenth centuries.

Hernández published his first poem, "Pastoril," in the pages of the weekly *El Pueblo de Orihuela* in January, 1930; others soon appeared in various local and regional papers. By June of that year the "shepherd poet of Orihuela" had begun to occasion a certain amount of favorable—albeit regional—critical attention. The literary activity of the whole group increased: they published their first magazine, gave public readings, organized an active theatrical group, even a soccer team.

II *Madrid 1931–32*

All too soon, Miguel decided that he was ready for a greater challenge: Madrid. "Miguel Hernández had full confidence in his talent," José Martínez Arenas remembers. "He didn't doubt that he would triumph as soon as he arrived in Madrid. Ignoring the advice of his friends, who were far from sharing his optimism, he set forth."[5] The six months which Miguel spent in Madrid (December, 1931–May, 1932) were difficult for him: he was timid, and yet he had continually to promote himself. He was nearly destitute, and unable to find a job. He had trouble adjusting to the ways and the noises of the city; the literary circles did not open to him. Several years later, he wrote about this experience:

> Alto soy de mirar a las palmeras,
> rudo de convivir con las montañas. . .
> Yo me vi bajo y blando en las aceras
> de una ciudad espléndida de arañas.
> Difíciles barrancos de escaleras,
> calladas cataratas de ascensores,
> ¡qué impresión de vacío!,
> ocupaban el puesto de mis flores,
> los aires de mis aires y mi río.[6]
> ("El silbo de afirmación en la aldea")

> I am tall from looking at palm trees,
> Coarse from living with the mountains. . .
> I saw myself small and soft on the sidewalks
> Of a city resplendent with chandeliers.
> Difficult canyons of stairs,
> Hushed cataracts of elevators—
> What an impression of emptiness!—
> Were standing in stead of my flowers,
> The whistling of my winds and my river.
> ("The Whistling Song of Affirmation in the Village")

Most of Hernández's biographer-critics believe that this visit was beneficial. Both Puccini and Ramos cite and agree with Cano Ballesta's assessment: "In this time he was truly able to take the pulse of the literary life in Madrid and to comprehend the significance of the Gongorine movement" (1st ed., 1962, p. 25). This affirmation seems questionable, for the Neo-Gongorine movement, with its hermetic, heavily metaphoric and syntactically difficult verse, had peaked some five years earlier. Gerardo Diego's book of verse in the Neo-Gongorine style, *Fábula de Equis y Zeda* (published 1932) may quite possibly have impressed Hernández as an individual book, but certainly the movement itself was dead. Indeed, Cano Ballesta revises his own assessment in the second edition of his book, inserting a qualification: ". . . he could . . . comprehend—although somewhat tardily—the significance of the Neo-Gongorine [note change of name] movement and all the poetry of the Generation of 1927" (p. 25).

How then do we explain Miguel's poetic activity after his return to Orihuela: why did he begin composing the *décimas* (poems of ten octosyllabic verses, rhyming *abbaaccddc*) of his *Expert in Moons* in the Neo-Gongorine style if it was so clearly passé? He did so, as Ramos points out, not because of the poetic climate in Madrid, but because of Ramón Sijé, whose influence on Miguel appears to have increased after the chastened "shepherd poet" returned from Madrid. Such deepened ties are perfectly comprehensible, for Sijé recognized Miguel's brilliance and offered him a noble outlet for his talent: Miguel was to write in the service of the regenerated Faith, the "lyrical, not normative" Catholicism (Vivanco, p. 503) which Sijé championed. Given Sijé's well-known predilection for the Baroque and his conception of metaphor as "the very center of poetry" (quoted in Cano Ballesta, p. 17, n. 12), the style he urged on Miguel was (passé or not) the Neo-Gongorine.

The sustained poetic effort which resulted in Miguel's first book, *Expert in Moons*, and in a number of other poems—those groups labeled "Octavas" (a poem of eight hendecasyllabic lines) and "Décimas" (pp. 49–56 and 165–73, respectively) in the *Complete Works*—consumed the rest of 1932 (Puccini, p. 158). With the financial backing of Don Luis Almarcha and José Martínez Arenas, he was able to have *Expert in Moons* published in January, 1933. He and Sijé traveled to various literary clubs in the province; Sijé lectured, Miguel read his poetry. In support of our thesis that Miguel's work was very nearly directed by Sijé is the following notice from the Alicante newspaper *El Luchador*, May 2, 1933: "Last Saturday two young and interesting Orihuelan writers occupied the podium of our atheneum: Ramón Sijé and Miguel Hernández Giner. Sijé . . . affirmed . . . the dance as a cosmic attitude, the Baroque as a model for behavior. . . . He defined the metaphor, following a line from Góngora to Guillén, as the very heart of poetry, reading at the end of his brilliant lecture some verses of *Expert in Moons*, conceived in accordance with the theories he had expounded" (quoted in Cano Ballesta, p. 17, n. 12).

The period 1933–34 is one of experimentation in Hernández's work. He seems to have left the Neo-Gongorine style behind him, turning from its aestheticism and preoccupation with metaphor to a more thematic poetry, typified in the "Silbos" ("Whistles") and in other "bucolic-evangelical" (Puccini) poems. The miracle play *How You've Changed!* was written during this period and is clearly similar to this religious verse. It was during this year, while visiting mutual friends, that Hernández met García Lorca, with whom he corresponded from time to time. And he met Josefina Manresa, who was to become his fiancée, his wife, the mother of his sons, and his widow. She inspired a number of love sonnets in this period.

III The Second Stay in Madrid

In March, 1934, Hernández decided he was ready to try Madrid once again. Considerably more mature this time, he brought with him a published book, the manuscript of his miracle play, and the first drafts of another book of poetry tentatively entitled *La imagen de tu huella (The Image of Your Footprint)*. It would be retitled *El silbo vulnerado (The Grievéd Whistling)* before being published as *The Unending Thunderbolt*. His reception this time in the capital was also far different. José Bergamín immediately agreed to publish *How You've Changed!* in his prestigious Neo-Catholic magazine, *Cruz y Raya*. Simultaneously the literary world seemed to open to Hernández: he soon counted among his friends the poets and intellectuals Rafael Alberti, María Teresa León, Luis Cernuda, María Zambrano, Luis Felipe Vivanco, Manuel Altolaguirre, Antonio Aparicio, and most influential of all, Pablo Neruda. Within the year he met and became friends with Vicente Aleixandre, who with Neruda was to inspire and preside over a radical change in Miguel's poetry.

In 1935, Hernández resolved his economic difficulties by accepting a job with José María de Cossío, who was editing a taurine encyclopedia to be published by Espasa-Calpe. Otherwise the year was a turbulent one for Miguel. Passionately in love with Josefina, he was driven to desperation by her typical provincial reserve: she neither surrendered herself emotionally to him in her letters, nor would she give herself sexually to him on the few occasions when he was able to return to Orihuela. The beautiful sonnets of *The Unending Thunderbolt* grew out of the torment of this period.

He loved and hated Madrid by turns, feeling closer to Josefina and Orihuela the more he felt alienated in the city. He wrote to her in April, 1935: "Here one can perceive nothing: one moves like a somnambulist, removed from time and from all of the best things of this earth. If only you knew how I hate Madrid! Sleeping in a strange bed, dealing with people who neither interest you nor care for you, eating not what you'd like, but what you're given. . . . And then, this constant jumble of cars, streetcars, exhaust fumes, people that jostle you on every corner, streets in which the sun only shines out of obligation. And then what I miss most: YOU, your company, your voice, your quarrels, your five- or six-year-old's mistrust, your eyes where I see myself small and far away, your hands which warmed mine. . . . When will I stop being here?" (Zardoya, *Miguel Hernández*, p. 20). Yet a few weeks later he had changed utterly: "It seems to me that I am not the man you need. . . . I have my life here in Madrid, it would be impossible for me to live in Orihuela now; [here] I have friends who comprehend me perfectly, there no one understands me and no one cares about anything I do. . ." (Zardoya, *Miguel Hernández*, p. 21, n. 67). Josefina's "exaggerated chastity bordering on prudishness," as Ifach puts it (p. 140), drove Miguel to desperation; after a few months in the freer atmosphere of Madrid he could bear it even less. For almost a year their relationship would be strained, their letters perfunctory.

IV *Political Activism*

The friends who understood him so well were slowly changing the naive young man from Orihuela. Hernández had never been interested in politics, but in the feverishly political atmosphere of Madrid in 1935, and surrounded as he was by activists like Alberti, María Teresa León, and Neruda, he could no longer remain aloof. Raúl González Tuñón writes: "About this time Miguel used to listen very attentively as we discussed with our friends . . . the double function of poetry in periods of disruption, of transition; in revolutionary periods. One day Miguel Hernández declared himself to be resolutely on our side. He knew, as we did, that we were in the maelstrom."[7] The play *Sons of Stone* (in the style of Lope de Vega), several poems, and one prose piece "Verano e invierno" ("Summer and Winter," pp. 941–42) attest to Miguel's conversion to the ranks of committed artists.

His poetic evolution was no less startling and was in fact related to his political and religious changes. Miguel's elemental, often volcanic sentiments were ill-matched to the measured and classical form of the sonnet: that he effected their synthesis in *The Unending Thunderbolt* is one of the greatest testimonies of his genius. Far more suited to his sentiments and nature, as he discovered in this year of change, were the longer, unrhymed verses of Aleixandre and Neruda, which he soon began to emulate. These two poets also represented a new freedom in the choice of themes, symbols, and vocabulary: Aleixandre with the Surrealist's oneiric lack of inhibition, Neruda with his new poetics of the ordinary, of the "impure." Both represented a break with the "pure" poetry championed by Juan Ramón Jiménez and written (for a number of years at least) by the poets of the Generation of 1927. Neruda founded a literary magazine—*Caballo Verde para la Poesía* (*A Green Horse for Poetry*)—as a "paladin for impure poetry" (Zardoya, *Miguel Hernández*, p. 23). In the first issue (October, 1935), Neruda's Prologue-Manifest read (in part): "Let the poetry that we seek be thus, worn as if with acid by the tasks of the hand, impregnated with sweat and fumes, smelling of urine and of lilies, splattered with the various excesses that are committed within and without the law. A poetry as impure as a dress, as a body, with food stains, and shameful positions, with wrinkles . . ." (Cano Ballesta, pp. 283–84).

Hernández publicly declared his enthusiasm for Neruda's type of poetry (as opposed to that of Juan Ramón Jiménez) in his review of the Chilean's first *Residencia en la tierra* (*Residence on the Earth*): "I am sick of so much art in a minor key, pure art. The disordered and chaotic confusion of the Bible, where I see great spectacles, cataclysms, is what stirs me. . . . What bores me is the tiny delicate voice that becomes ecstatic at the sight of a poplar, shoots off four little verses and believes that everything has then been done in poetry. Enough of this cloying prissiness from poets who are like confectionary nuns, all nicety, all sugar-coated fingertips" (Guerrero Zamora, pp. 78–79).

Slowly, Neruda's irreverent position toward everything tradi-

tional began to leave its mark on Miguel, who had been attempting
to maintain—against all the incursions of the new ideas in the
capital—his friendship with and belief in Sijé. Neruda openly
expressed his dislike for Sijé's magazine in a letter (dated August 18,
1935) to Miguel: "Congratulations on not having quarreled with
Gallo Crisis, but it will surely come in time. You're too healthy
[sane] to put up for long with that soutanic-satanic stench" (Zardoya,
Miguel Hernández, p. 23). The Chilean was right: when Miguel
published his Surrealist "Vecino de la muerte" ("Neighbor of
Death") in the first issue of *Caballo Verde,* it precipitated a definitive break with Sijé, who wrote to Miguel, scandalized, on
November 29:

> It is terrible not to have sent me *Caballo Verde.* . . . Although of course
> *Caballo Verde* shouldn't interest me much. There is no trace in it of poetic
> fury, nor of polemical fury. Impure and sectarian horse . . . . The one who
> is suffering a great deal is you, Miguel. Someday I will blame *someone* for
> your present human-poetic sufferings. A terrible and cruel transformation.
> The reading of your poem "Mi sangre es un camino" ["My Blood is a Road"]
> tells me everything. Truly, a road of melancholy horses. But not the road of
> a man, not the road of human dignity. Nerudism (how disgusting! Pablo and
> the forest, a narcissistic and subhuman ritual of groins, of soft little hairs in
> forbidden parts and of forbidden horses!); Aleixandrism, Albertism. (Zar-
> doya, *Miguel Hernández,* pp. 23–24)

Miguel never answered Sijé's letter, for within the month, entirely unexpectedly, the twenty-three-year-old Sijé was dead. Shak-
en deeply—but too far committed to his new world to turn back—
Miguel wrote his moving "Elegy" for Sijé. He was able to have it
included in *The Unending Thunderbolt,* which went to press in late
January, 1936. With the publication of this book, the first period of
Miguel's production ended; the shepherd-poet had grown up.

V *Early Works*

The works which constitute this first period include thirty-one
short prose pieces[8] (varying in length between a hundred and nine
hundred words), most of which were first published by Hernández
in various provincial newspapers. Of the thirteen which are dated
(by Hernández or by date of publication), twelve were written between 1930 and 1935. The others we may assume to be contem-

poraneous, given the similarity of their style and subject matter. Reminiscent of Miró, these pieces (like much of the prose of Miró and of Juan Ramón Jiménez) grew out of the Modernist urge to "conquer prose as a pure poetic instrument" (Cano Ballesta, "La prosa poética . . .," p. 267). The first piece is an elegy to Miró, and it is dedicated to the other master of the genre, Juan Ramón.

The pieces are markedly similar in vocabulary, syntax, and subject matter to the poetry of this first period. Most are poetic descriptions, often with dialogue, of the life and countryside where Miguel grew up. Judging them in retrospect, one can only feel that they were experiments for Miguel, falling between the poetry he was writing and the miracle play. Bruna Cinti asserts that these prose works (which Ramos calls "poems in prose") are so close to being poetry that generic distinctions are almost nonexistent. To substantiate this, she scans the "Elegy to Miró" as poetry and finds it to be composed entirely of hepta- and hendecasyllabic lines.[9]

The poetry written in this first period includes the following books and poems collected in the *Complete Works:* the two published volumes *Expert in Moons* and *The Unending Thunderbolt;* the "Poems of Adolescence" and "Other Poems 1933–34"; the sonnets written for *The Image of Your Footprint* and *The Grievéd Whistling* but not included in *The Unending Thunderbolt;* and "Other Poems 1935–36." This final group of twelve poems (to which we should add "Alba de hachas" ["Dawn of the Hatchets"], finally published in the *Complete Poetic Works,* pp. 280–81), written during Miguel's second stay in Madrid, are transitional in his work: their themes and symbols place them in the first period, but their style is that of the second. Lamentably, much of Hernández's youthful poetry was left out of the *Complete Works.* Some sixty poems have since been published piecemeal in a variety of books and journals (Couffon collected over forty in his study): all of these are now available in the *Complete Poetic Works.*

Hernández also wrote two works for the theater in this period: *How You've Changed!* and *Sons of Stone.*[10] *Sons* is transitional (like the aforementioned dozen poems), but since its theme and symbols are more closely related to those of the second period and since in form it resembles the wartime *The Comeliest Peasant,* we shall consider it in the next chapter.

Beginning with the formal or structural aspects of the work of this period, we find that genre, form, and style distinguish it from later work. The prose pieces constitute a genre unique to this first period; later prose writings are polemical and/or theoretical. The miracle play is also unique in Hernández's *oeuvre:* although he wrote other plays, he never again attempted to follow the rigid conventions of this allegorical genre, established by Calderón in the seventeenth century. It is interesting to note that nearly all of the "traditional" verse[11] which Hernández wrote in the first period was for this highly conventional play: *romances* (octosyllabic verses with assonance in the even-numbered lines), *romancillos* (similar assonance in six- or seven-syllable verses), *seguidillas* (quatrains of alternating hepta- and pentasyllabic verses with even-numbered lines assonant), *letrillas* (rondelets), *redondillas* (octosyllabic quatrains rhyming *abba* or *abab*), and *quintillas* (five octosyllabic lines with two rhymes). Mixed with these were the cultured forms that Hernández was using in most of his poetry at that time: *décimas*, *silvas* (freely alternating hepta- and hendecasyllabic verses, some rhymed, some assonant), and *octavas reales* (hendecasyllabic octaves, rhyming variously in the first six lines: *abbaba* or *abbaab* or *ababba*, ending *cc*).

The poetry of Hernández's first period is easily distinguished by its structure from his later work. The forms which predominate—and subsequently disappear from his poetry—are cultured or Italianate: *octavas reales, décimas,* sonnets in the style of Garcilaso, *liras, silvas* or *canciones* and other combinations of hepta- and hendecasyllabic lines account for approximately two hundred thirty of the two hundred sixty poems. The traditional form *par excellence* in Spanish poetry is the octosyllabic *romance;* we find less than a dozen octosyllabic compositions in this first period. The remaining poems vary greatly: those collected by Claude Couffon show the influence of Rubén Darío with ten-, twelve-, fourteen-, and sixteen-syllable verses; there are some very early examples of free verse in *arte menor* (poetry with octosyllabic or shorter verses). In eight of the thirteen poems which I have labeled transitional, Hernández had begun experimenting with combinations of seven-, eleven-, and fourteen-, or eleven-, and fourteen-syllable lines. He was to use these combinations extensively in the poetry of the war years.

In his early choice of genres and poetic forms, then, Hernández demonstrated his attachment to and dependence upon tradition. According to Northrop Frye, the very essence of the *auto sacramental* is that it is directed to an audience which accepts the story without question; moreover, it concerns ideals which all members of the audience consider to be desirable (*Anatomy,* pp. 288–89). Such conventionality is natural in a young poet, for as Pedro Salinas writes, "In spiritual history tradition is the natural habitat of the poet. He is born, poetically, within tradition; in it he finds the air to breathe, and he advances through its space toward the fulfillment of his creative destiny."[12] It is even more natural in a largely self-educated provincial who found imitation the best way to learn the art of writing.

VI   *Vocabulary*

The vocabulary Hernández used in this early prose and poetry is far more recondite than in any other period, attesting to the influence of the conceptist poets—especially Góngora—whom he was imitating. Rubén Darío's poetry, which so clearly inspired the poems collected by Couffon, also boasts a difficult vocabulary. Yet Hernández's lexicon coincides only rarely with Darío's or Góngora's, for like them he was interested in the minting of new words and in the recognition and elevation to poetry of new (or heretofore unperceived) beauties. Moreover, Hernández lacked the wide classical education of a Góngora or a Darío: while he used Latinisms or mythological and Biblical references, they were never abundant in his work. Some *culterano* or Latinate words found in this early verse include a number which are direct imitations from specific Golden Age poets, such as "vadear" (to ford), "manida" (den), and "Aminadab" (a Biblical name) from St. John of the Cross; "holanda espuma" (chambray froth), "mordaza" (gag), "medoros" and "angélicas" (the name of two lovers who inspired one of Góngora's most famous poems, "La fábula de Angélica y Medoro"). It is frequent in Hernández to find names written without a capital letter; proper nouns are thus transformed into generic nouns or adjectives: "bákeres más viudas" ("more widowed bakers," p. 68, referring to the famous black dancer, Josephine Baker, to describe black weathervanes); "mendigos/niños, moiseses" ("beggar children, moseses," p. 63). This is a rather typical use of poetic tradition for Hernández: patterned roughly after the *culteranos* like Góngora and Quevedo and the Modernist Rubén Darío with their extensive classical allusions, yet with a touch of originality, for his models very rarely lexicalized (or made generic) the proper nouns which they used.

Hernández's early work abounds in neologisms which are perhaps the modern equivalent of Latinisms. Most of them are impossible to translate, but a few of the simpler ones are "lunarse" (to "moonify," for reaching sexual maturity), "rascaleches" (literally, "milkscrapers," but with obscene implications, used to describe the menacingly sterile skyscrapers—*rascacielos*—he saw in Madrid), "guardalápidas" ("gravestone guard," for a cemetery watchman).[13]

Another characteristic of Hernández's vocabulary in this period which derived from his Golden Age models is his use of "extrapoetic" or nonpoetic words: vulgarities, prosaisms, slang. When he later began to imitate Neruda's frequent ruptures in semantic systems it would not be very different from inserting an image like "la sierpe en mangas de camisa" ("the snake in its shirtsleeves," p. 105) within a classic *silva*, or "una noche oscura de sartenes" ("a night dark with frying pans," p. 218) in a Petrarchan love sonnet. Yet it is perhaps surprising that there is not more of this class of words, considering the lowly nature of his subject matter: barbers, lizards, taverns, washerwomen, outhouses, udders, wells, watermelons, to mention a few subjects of the poems in *Expert in Moons*.

It is only in this first period that we find examples of dialect in Hernández's work.[14] There are two poems written entirely in Murcian, the regional patois: "Al verla muerta" ("Upon Seeing Her Dead," *Complete Poetic Works*, pp. 489–90) and "En mi barraquica" ("In My Little Hut"; *Hispania*, 55 [1972], 344–45). Others ("Postrer Sueño," "Last Dream," and "Nocturna," "Nocturne," *Complete Poetic Works*, pp. 513–15, 490–92) contain dialogues in Murcian. Additionally, we find regional words scattered throughout his early work. Manuel Alvar has studied a number of Miguel's regionalisms in his article on dialecticisms in twentieth-century Spanish poetry; some are vulgarisms, some are Aragonese words which have been kept alive in southeastern Spain, others are specifically Murcian. "We observe that these are always words of a very concrete nature, rural terms which give this poetry—so often an imitation of the classics—a transparent value [efficacy] of lived reality."[15]

It is most clearly in the syntax of Hernández's early works that we see the influence of the Golden Age poets. He embraced such *culterano* devices as hyperbaton (an extreme disruption of normal sentence order, e.g., "red the have you seen roses" instead of "have you seen the red roses?" which may serve to emphasize the misplaced words—red, in our example—or otherwise modify the basic statement), using at least six of the different types of hyperbaton which Dámaso Alonso adduces to Góngora in *La lengua poética de*

Góngora.[16] Let us consider a few examples (which sound no more natural in Spanish than in English):

> Por el arco, contra los picadores,
> del cuerno, flecha, a dispararme parto. (p. 61)

> Through the bow, at the picadors,
> Of the horn, arrow, to shoot myself I depart.

This means: I depart like an arrow to shoot myself through the bow of [formed by] the horns at the picadors.

> por esta, donde tiene, serranía
> tanta, pura la luz, categoría. (p. 63)

> Through this, where it has, mountain range
> So much, pure the light, quality.

It should read: through this mountain range where the pure light has so much quality.

In addition to hyperbaton, Hernández imitated the Baroque devices of *plurimembración* (the construction of a sentence or a phrase with two or more syntactically identical fragments; e.g., "sin pecado, sin cólera, sin prisa" [p. 105], "Without sin, without anger, without haste"); parallelism (a sentence with parallel phrases or clauses; e.g., "creciendo en paz y madurando en guerra" [p. 90], "Growing in peace and maturing in war"); correlation and correspondence (a point-by-point relationship between a series of, for example, substantives at the beginning of a poem and adjectives at the end); e.g.,

> Yo, dios y adán, que lo cultivo (*a*) y riego (*b*)
> por mi mano (*a*₁) y conducto . . . (*b*₁) (p. 89)

> I, god and adam, who cultivate (*a*) and water (*b*) it
> With my hand (*a*₁) and conduit . . . (*b*₁)

We also find examples of *recolección*, the reiteration or recapitulation of a series:[17]

> Vierto la red (*a*), esparzo la semilla (*b*)
> entre ovas aguas (*a*₁), surcos y amapolas (*b*₁),
> sembrando a secas (*b*₂) y pescando a solas (*a*₂) . . . (p. 225)

> I cast the net (a), scatter the seed (b)
> Amongst seaweed, waters (a_1), furrows and poppies (b_1),
> Sowing only (b_2) and fishing alone (a_2) . . .

He used several lexical formulas typical of Góngora, including the well-known "A, si no B" (A, if not B). This form, as in "testimonio primero/del abril, si no agente" ("First testimony of April, if not [its] agent," p. 87), affirms the first assertion A, and denies the second, B. Yet by mentioning B somewhat equivocally, it insinuates that perhaps B is true as well. Thus the reader is provoked into considering the whole phrase more carefully.

Hernández was a *conceptista* as well as a *culterano:* that is, he not only used Latinate diction as the *culterano* Góngora had, but also the brilliantly elaborate conceits (*conceptos*) for which the *conceptista* Quevedo was known (in actuality the two styles overlapped in both Golden Age poets as well). The early works abound in elaborate conceits and ingenious images: *Expert in Moons* seems an exercise book of imagery; the miracle play is one long sustained metaphor. Hernández deliberately sought to make *Expert* as hermetic as possible, going so far as to delete the descriptive titles of the poems, without which some of them are genuinely impenetrable. So obscure are they, in fact, that one of Hernández's most eminent critics, Concha Zardoya, misinterpreted at least five of them, as we can see by comparing their titles, only recently discovered by Cano Ballesta (pp. 61–62, n. 5), with Zardoya's analyses of the poems in *Poesía española contemporánea* (p. 650). Beyond the fact of the suppression of titles, in a short essay recently discovered by Leopoldo de Luis, there is further proof that Hernández assiduously cultivated this hermeticism. Responding to the (self-posed?) question "What is a Poem?", Hernández wrote:

A beautiful affected lie. An insinuated truth. Simply insinuating it, a truth doesn't seem a lie. A truth as precious and recondite as that of the mine. One must be a miner of poems to see in their ethiopias of shadows their indias of lights. . . . The poem cannot present itself to us venuslike or naked. Naked poems are the anatomy of poems. And is there anything more horrible than a skeleton? Preserve, poets, the secret of the poem: sphinxlike. Let them learn to tear it away like the bark from a tree. . . . Except in the case of prophetic poetry for which clarity is essential—because [with such poetry] it is not a question of illustrating sensations, or of dazzling the mind with the flashes of the perfectly tailored image, but rather of spreading emotions, of inflaming lives—, guard, poets, against giving fruits without skins, seas without salt. . . .[18]

After those early years, Miguel never again sought to write anything which could be labeled "a beautiful affected lie," never again resorted to such artificial syntax. If the works of his last two periods have anything in common, it is precisely their presentation "venuslike or nude" of the simple skeleton of truth.

To summarize our consideration of the formal aspect of Hernández's early work: (1) the miracle play and the poetic prose are genres unique to this period. His use of the *auto sacramental* and of the cultivated verse forms favored by the Golden Age poets shows his dependence upon tradition. (2) He used a vocabulary unlike that of his later periods. (3) His syntax, in general modeled on that of the Golden Age poets, was frequently elaborate and artificial, designed to cloak the "precious and recondite" truth of the poem.

VII *Content*

Moving into the material or "content" aspect of Miguel's early work, it is no surprise to find that his favorite tropes, or figures of speech, are allusion, elaborate metaphors, and conceptist images or conceits. Also important are personification and other related transformations, some of which are listed by Concha Zardoya: dynamization, animalization, vegetalization, and personification of the inert, of the astral, and of the incorporeal; concretization, corporealization and/or liquification of the abstract—the inert (pp. 661–62). While Zardoya draws no general conclusions from this list, it is evident that these transformations all tend to make the transformed object more tangible or commonplace, and thereby more comprehensible or affective to the reader.

Bruna Cinti mentions another lexical formula of Hernández's which has a similar effect. It is the linking of some common verb of action (return, come, go, go back) by a preposition to an abstract or concrete substantive which always seems anomalous in the resulting context.[19] Some examples: "Vienen de los esfuerzos sobrehumanos / y van a la canción, y van al beso" (p. 227; "They return from superhuman efforts / They go to the song and they go to the kiss"); "me querello / tanto de tanto andar de fiera en fiera / sangre" (p. 222; "I complain / So much of so much walking from savage to savage / Blood"); "De sangre en sangre vengo" and "llego de amapola en amapola / a dar en la cornada de mi sino. / Criatura hubo que vino / desde la sementera de la nada . . ." (p. 239; "From blood to blood I come," "I arrive from poppy to poppy / To hit the bull's horn's thrust that is my fate. / Once there was a child who came / From the seed-bed of nothingness . . ."). Both this formula and the general tendency to concretize or personify the abstract continue through all the phases of Hernández's work. This, along with his exaltation of the physical, is part of what many critics refer to as Hernández's "earthiness," for many his most outstanding characteristic.[20]

The figures of speech which predominate in this early period attest to Hernández's cleverness and to his technical virtuosity. Allusion (one form of which we have already mentioned in the study of Hernández's vocabulary), especially to classical figures, is important in the earliest works:

> Homeros de dolor, los ruy-señores . . . (p. 104)
> (Homers of pain, the nightingales . . .)
>
> Medusa vegetal, la vid rodea . . . (p. 117)
> (Vegetal Medusa, the vine encircles . . .)
>
> [Of a barber:] Blanco narciso por obligación . . . . (p. 65)
> (White narcissus by obligation . . .)

Metaphors, sometimes trite—as in the sonnet "Es tu boca . . ." (*Complete Poetic Works*, pp. 515–16; "Your Mouth Is . . .") where the lover's mouth is described in thirteen clichéd metaphors[21]—but more frequently audacious and conceptist, are central to the earliest poetry, and continue to characterize his work through all periods. A few examples (from *Expert in Moons*): an undertaker: "the final tailor, of glass and pine" (XXXVI); udders: "granaries of whiteness, founts of moons" (XXXIII); weathervanes: "dancers grafted onto Christian vertices" (XXIV); bullfighters: "imprudent emulators of lizards, backs resplendent with colors" (III); lemon blossom: "arctic flower southbound: your slippage is required for the progress of the canary [lemon]" (XXV).

The frequency and type of metaphor begin to change after *Expert* and the miracle play, and similes are used more commonly: "Como el toro he nacido para el luto" (p. 226; "Like the bull I was born for mourning"); "me desespero / como si fuera un huracán de lava" (p. 224; "I grow desperate / As if I were a hurricane of lava"). The change in the metaphors themselves can best be described with Carlos Bousoño's terminology.[22] Hernández's earliest poetry is filled with "traditional" metaphors, in which vehicle (e.g., rubies) and tenor (lips) have some objective quality in common (in our example, color:

rubies and lips are both red). In the later poetry of the first period—still traditional in form and subject matter—Hernández has begun to use what Bousoño calls "visionary" metaphors and "visions." In the visionary metaphor, vehicle and tenor have little or no objective similarity. They are related subjectively; both should evoke the same emotion in the reader. For example, when Hernández writes,

> Un carnívoro cuchillo
> de ala dulce y homicida
> sostiene un vuelo y un brillo
> alrededor de mi vida. (p. 213)

> A carnivorous knive
> Of sweet and homicidal wing
> Sustains a flight and a brightness
> All about my life.

he is describing his heart. The image of a phantasmagorically hovering knife produces in him the same sense of dread, of tragic fatalism, as does the image of his (ill-fated) heart. Objectively, of course, the two images have nothing in common.

A "vision" is an image in which unreal qualities or functions are attributed to an object or person (as Bousoño notes, our definition of a metaphor has to be stretched to accommodate this figure of speech). Visions become increasingly important in Hernández's work beginning with *Thunderbolt*, peaking in the war years, diminishing in the last period. A few examples:

> Exasperado llego hasta la cumbre
> de tu pecho de isla, y lo rodeo
> de un ambicioso mar y un pataleo
> de exasperados pétalos de lumbre . . . (p. 227)

> Exasperated, I reach the summit
> Of your island breast, and I surround it
> With an ambitious sea and a kicking
> Of exasperated petals of fire.

> En mis manos levanto una tormenta
> de piedras, rayos y hachas estridentes
> sedienta de catástrofes y hambrienta. (p. 230)

In my hands I raise a storm
Of rocks, lightning, and strident axes,
[A storm] thirsting for catastrophes and starving.

Many of the poems of *Expert in Moons* are examples of the use of conceit (elaborate, extensively developed metaphors). Perhaps the best single example of this Baroque trope is the poem "Abril—*gongorino*" ("April—*Gongorine*," p. 47), which in its very title acknowledges its debt to one of the Golden Age masters of conceit. This poem maintains a metaphorical relationship between spring's inroads on the Valencian (Moorish) countryside and the campaigns of El Cid against the Moors. Its metaphorical density is matched by its verbal complexity, for the poem is studded with Hernández's puns and neologisms.

VIII   *Themes*

There is a greater variety of themes and/or subject matter (since much of the poetry and most of the prose in this period is purely descriptive, it cannot strictly be said to have themes) in these works than in Hernández's later writing. This is certainly due in part to the variety and quantity of writers whom he imitated—in theme as well as style—while young. When writing in the style of Rubén Darío, for example, Hernández emulated Darío's choice of exotic subject matter as well, writing about sultans and houris (see especially the poems of Couffon's collection). The "Ode to Vicente Aleixandre" imitates not only that poet's vocabulary and syntax, but also deals with one of his favorite themes—the sea. Similarly, the Miró-inspired prose pieces are about the local countryside and characters, as were Miró's; the miracle play treats the ideas of Temptation and of man's Fall, so common in Golden Age allegorical drama. In later years, Hernández's themes were inspired by personal circumstances, and he abandoned the mimeticism which accounts for much of the early variety.

The principal themes of this period may be grouped for purposes of analysis around the framework of the Great Mother archetype (as outlined in Chapter 1). I have distinguished and listed six major thematic groupings (although, as will become clear, these divisions are not strict), with some theoretical explanation, in the order in which they appear and become dominant in Hernández's work.

1. The vegetative, agricultural world, with its seasonal rhythms and its plastic variety; Nature, the Great Earth Mother, principally benevolent.[23] (Psychologically, this theme reflects the nascent ego's passive dependence on and acceptance of the Great Mother as nurturer.)

2. The phallic or genital theme, which Pablo Luis Ávila analyzes in his article on "the round and the piercing" in Hernández's work.[24] "The child passes through a stage in which the sexualization of the objects in the world around him achieves a pre–eminent place in his psyche," Ávila writes (p. 153).

3. Mortality or transitoriness (wherein the youth sees death all around him in nature; he associates his own fate with that of ephemeral flowers and insects). Berns writes that the poet sees "a real world in which mutability, transformations and boundlessness are of particular significance" (p. 59); Hernández's poetic vision is one "in which the cyclical quality of natural forces plays a prominent role" (p. 36).

4. The ambivalent desire to surrender to the unconscious, to give in to the temptations—sex, drink, suicide—which assail him, even though it means the extinction of his precarious self. Various critics of Hernández have remarked tendencies to self-destruction in his work. These may take the form of merging with nature: pantheism, hilozoism, or being "joined in the cosmos through sexual participation both literally and figuratively" (Rogers, p. 77). Others speak of his constant urge to commit suicide.[25] Javier Herrero ("Miguel Hernández: sangre y guerra," *Symposium*, 22, No. 2 [Summer 1968], 144–52) sees Hernández driven to a union—at first sexual, then political—which is "surrender" and the "sacrifice of [his] ego, . . . the crucifixion of [his] individual existence" (p. 148).

5. The solar/chthonic struggle, or the struggle between light and darkness, spirit and flesh. (This is simply a later stage of the struggle with the forces of the unconscious; the youth now identifies his consciousness or spiritual potential with the sun. He realizes that he must pit his "solar" masculinity—the power of thought, rationality, spirituality—against the insidious pull of the unconscious, which appeals to his phallic or chthonic masculinity.) For a time Hernández understands and expresses this conflict in religious terms, in the tradition of St. Paul. *How You've Changed!* is illustrative of this. It is Marie Chevallier's provocative thesis that Hernández's characteristic fatalism grew out of the realization that his God-given body was

impure by nature, that God had in other words predestined him to sin.[26] However, by the time of Miguel's second stay in Madrid the struggle has lost all moral overtones. The poems of *The Unending Thunderbolt* show his rationality under siege not only by sexual passion but also by continuous frustration of that passion.

6. Recognition of a personal, tragic fate. (As the youth matures he realizes that his fate is not as inevitable or as simple as a flower's; it is personal and vindictive.) This theme appears during the transition period, when Miguel stops using symbolic figures like the bull to represent his fate and speaks instead in the first person of his "bloody fate." Many critics consider this tragic fatalism to be Hernández's single greatest theme.

In our introductory sketch of Hernández's trajectory we mentioned the universal concerns—sex, death, love, and the desire for immortality—which endure throughout his production. In this first period sex is equated with lust, as exemplified in the numerous poems with phallic or orgiastic themes, such as "El adolescente" ("The Adolescent," p. 41); IV, X, XI, XII, and XL of *Expert in Moons;* "Égloga—*nudista*" ("Eclogue—*Nudist,*" pp. 99–100); "Me llamo barro . . ." ("I Call Myself Mud . . . ," pp. 220–22). Death is regarded with a fatalistic melancholy—both in the earliest poems when the transitoriness of the world and its creatures suggested Miguel's own fate to him ("Diario de junio—*interrumpido*" ["Diary of June—*Interrupted*"]; "Otoño—*mollar*" ["Autumn—*Ripe*"]; "Citación final" ["Final Appointment"]; "¡Y qué buena es la tierra de mi huerto!" ["Oh, How Good the Earth of My Garden!"]; "Como el toro . . ." ["Like the Bull . . ."]) and in the later poems of this period, when he spoke of his own bloody fate without circumlocution (Nos. 1, 2, 7, and 18 of *Thunderbolt;* "Sino sangriento" ["Bloody Fate"]; "Neighbor of Death"; "Me sobra el corazón" ["Heart to Spare"]). In *How You've Changed!* the redeemed man accepts death with religious equanimity: "Sea, Señor, cuando quiera / tu poder: a él me sujeto" ("Let it be, Lord, when your power / Decrees it; to it I subject myself," p. 578).

Love in the early work is directed toward the self (for the adolescent is extremely narcissistic) and in far lesser degree toward the opposite sex, which delights and obsesses the poet. It is only in a few poems of *Thunderbolt* that this generic love begins to be directed toward one woman, Josefina, to whom the book is dedicated ("To you alone, in fulfillment of a promise which you have probably forgotten, as if it were your own."). Even in *Thunderbolt* the majority of the "love" poems are about the lover/poet and his pain (1–6, 9, 10, 12, 13, 15, 16, 19, 20, 22, 23; and "Soneto Final" ["Final Sonnet"]), not about the beloved (exceptions: 8, 11, 21).

The desire for immortality or eternal return is rather subdued in the early work. Hernández's normal adolescent fatalism combined with his observations of Nature and her unpardoning cycles militate against belief in any reprieve from death. The most he aspires to is a sort of agricultural rebirth. This theme appears in the elegies to Ramón Sijé and to García Lorca and dominates the surreal "Neighbor of Death" (see below, p. 128.)

IX *Symbols and Motifs*

Once again we confront an abundance of data when we turn to the symbols of this early period. Hernández's diachronic development can be charted through a study of his symbols alone, so revealing are the changes they undergo from period to period. Here, however, we must necessarily be brief.[27] The symbols or motifs in a poet's work may be regarded as the component pieces, the concrete, if partial, representations of the larger concerns we have called themes. In Hernández the myriad symbols group themselves in a general way around the six archetypal themes just studied.

The agricultural/vegetative theme predominates in the earliest works, prose and poetry, which were often descriptive rather than symbolic or thematic. Frequently, then, such objects as flowers, birds, even bulls (all symbolic in later works) serve as models for pictorial descriptions in the beginning. The poet exults in the beauty of the world around him and tries, at first clumsily but then with increasing mastery, to transcribe this beauty into words:

> Las flores despiertan de su frío sueño
> abriendo a los besos del sol sus corolas;
> sobre los sembrados de verdor risueño
> florecen sangrientas miles de amapolas.
>
> El ruiseñor teje la canción primera;
> el límpido arroyo musical suspira . . .
> El vaho perfumado de la primavera
> en ráfagas cálidas por doquier se aspira. . . .
> ("¡Marzo viene . . . !"   *Complete Poetic Works,*
>   pp. 492–93)

The flowers awaken from their cold sleep
Opening corollas to the sun's kisses;
Over the sown fields of laughing green
Flower thousands of blood-red poppies.

The nightingale weaves the first song;
The limpid brook sighs melodically . . .
Warm gusts of the perfumed breath
Of spring are all o'er inhaled. ("March Is Coming . . . !")

Echa la luna en pandos aguaceros
vahos de luz que los árboles azulan
desde el éter goteado de luceros . . .
En las eras los grillos estridulan.

Con perfumes balsámicos, pululan
las brisas por el campo. En los senderos
los lagartos verdean y se ondulan
los reptiles agudos y rastreros. (p. 42)

In langorous showers the moon sends forth
From the heavens sprinkled with stars
Vapors of light which azure the trees. . .
In the garden the crickets stridulate.

With balsamic perfumes, the breezes pululate
Through the countryside. On the footpaths
The lizards turn green, and the sharp
Trailing reptiles undulate.

It is not long before the description of Mother Earth takes on
deeper thematic tones in Hernández's poetry. He begins to perceive her essential duplexities: she has two roles, container (or
womb) and nurturer (or transformer), each of which has positive and
negative aspects for the young man. A containing vessel may be
protective—as is a mother's womb—or it may be restrictive (even
suffocating), a prison, a tomb, an overprotective mother. Similarly,
the nurturer/transformer may feed him well, fostering his physical
and spiritual growth, or "feed" him noxious substances, causing his
physical or psychological death.

To represent the elementary containing character, Hernández
uses the symbols of water, trees (both of which contain and nourish),
gorges, pomegranates, circles, countryside and fields, rock, earth,

shadow, the moon, silence and calmness, the uroboros,[28] and various imprisoning vessels. There are far fewer representations of the positive nurturing or transformative role of the feminine: in addition to trees and water, bees and the motif of the eternal return are the only significant ones. The Mother's power to transform negatively (or destroy) is symbolized in axes, frogs or toads, and by animals with cloven hooves (*pezuñas*) or claws. The motif of the dissolution of the self through drunkennness or other forms of alienation may be included here (as well as in the next group).

The phallic/genital theme and that of Hernández's ambivalent feelings toward orgiastic (principally sexual) behavior are often represented by the same symbols. The genital poems precede the orgiastic ones: they describe numerous physical phenomena in genital terms (see Ávila). The orgiastic poems take this description a step further, attributing an animus to all the sexually charged phenomena: all work to arouse the young man's lust, which will then drive him into the fatal embrace with the unconscious. Rogers, who calls this theme "death in love," treats it extensively in his study (see especially pp. 56, 65–66, 72, 134). The principal symbols in this group are the plow (male); the furrow or earth (female); fire (lust, passion); lemons (breasts); figs (testicles) and the fig tree (masculinity, lust); the foot (phallus) and the act of walking (intromission); blood (repository of all unconscious urges, especially lust); snakes, palm trees, and fountains (all phallic); bulls (males); wind (passion); the rose (female); and the moon, which like Lorca's moon is a sexual excitant. The motifs of the sexual act as death and of lust in general are also part of this group.

The next group of symbols represents the theme of impermanence or transitoriness: the crow (foreboding death); and the bull (the male driven in spite of himself to an early death); the cicada or grasshopper (which lives but one short, strident season); spray or sea foam (which has no lasting substance); the moon (regulator, with the stars, of destiny, as in "Nacimos en mala luna," "We were born under an evil moon," p. 650); and the motifs of death, destiny, and the seasons.

The solar/chthonic conflict of the youth is reflected in the symbols of the almond tree; light (including the sun, lightning, firecrackers, flames); eyes (the windows of the soul, reflectors of the "higher" masculinity); and the seasons (winter is pure, spring is temptation, summer is sin). There are no symbols exclusively related to the last theme, which is the recognition of a personal fate. Instead Hernández transforms many of the earlier generic symbols, like the bull, into symbols for himself. The bull is no longer a fated creature symbolizing the world's impermanence: he now represents Miguel's personal fate.

Such, then, are the most important symbols of the first period. Some—the almond tree; the countryside and fields (as container and nurturer); the crow; the circle or wheel; the cicada; axes; lemons; frogs and toads; figs; snakes; the uroboros; and the motifs of lust, dissolution, and the seasons as moral presences—are exclusive to this period. Others appear in two periods, some in all three; some change tenor as Hernández matures, and others—true constants in his work—remain the same throughout.

X   Analysis of Symbols

Let us analyze a few of the more important first-period symbols before going on to consider some representative works. The almond tree blossoms weeks before any other flowering tree; it fades rapidly and thus sometimes symbolizes (as do various other flowers) the ephemeral: "A punto de ser flor y no ser nada / está tu flor, almendra" ("On the verge of being a flower and on the verge of nothingness / Lies your flower, almond," p. 129).[29] It has another, more important meaning in Hernández, however; its whiteness and fragility, antedating the luxuriant growth of the later spring, suggest youthful purity to the poet, a purity which will soon be tempted by the sin of summer and lost: "Flor de almendro temprano: / preliminar inocencia" ("Flower of the early almond tree: / Preliminary innocence," p. 167).

In the poem "Primera lamentación de la carne" ("First Lamentation of the Flesh," pp. 129–130) the symbol of the almond tree is used with the motif of the seasons to represent the young poet's struggles to maintain his besieged chastity. This poem is typical of many which deal with the solar/chthonic contest, most written in the intensely religious period of How You've Changed! Indeed, the first act of the play also centers around this theme and uses both the almond tree and the seasons. Act I is an allegory of the Man-Child's fall from a "State of Innocence": this state was to be represented on stage as "a field of whipped cream almond trees and snows" (p. 439).

The character Innocence (dressed as Froth or Spray), who makes a brief appearance in Act I, says of herself: I may be found "en cada almendro ante-verde" ("in every not-yet-green almond tree"), yet

> apenas flor me conozco
> en la rama principianta,
> cuando la almendra aprendiza
> con terciopelo me mata. (p. 451)

> Scarcely have I recognized myself as a flower
> On the neophyte branch,
> When the apprentice almond
> Kills me with its velvet.

In the play Desire is aroused by the springtime, and (literally) assails and routs Innocence, thus hastening the Man-Child's fall from Grace. The fall is represented in the following terms: "The almond trees, the snow, the clouds, begin to rain their symbolic purity with a terrifying din. Beginning with this scene and continuing until the last scene, the State of Innocence will be transforming itself into a corrupt paradise of fig and of apple trees, as well as all other sorts of sensuous trees" (p. 481).

Even a brief comparison of the foregoing to "First Lamentation of the Flesh" reveals how similarly Hernández treated the theme in verse.

> El sol ya panifica soledades:
> su luz es ya membruda.
> Y yo me altero ya bajo mi carne,
> bajo su dictadura.
> . . . .

> No seas, primavera; no te acerques,
> quédate en alma, almendro:
> sed tan sólo un propósito de verdes,
> de ser verdes sin serlo.

> Por qué os marcháis, espirituales fríos,
> eneros virtüosos,
> donde mis fuegos imposibilito
> y sereno mis ojos.
> . . . .

Oh Muerte, oh inmortal almendro cano:
mondo, pero florido,
sálvame de mi cuerpo y sus pecados,
mi tormento y mi alivio.

La desgracia del mundo, mi desgracia
entre los dedos tengo,
oh carne de orinar, activa y mala,
que haciéndome estás bueno.

The sun is now tilling the lonely places:
Its light is now robust.
And I am now changing beneath my flesh
Under its dictature.
. . . .
Be not, spring; come no closer,
Remain a soul, almond tree:
Be only a design for greenness,
For becoming green without being so.

Why are you leaving, spiritual cold,
Virtuous Januaries,
Where my fires cannot live
And my eyes are serene.
. . . .
Oh Death, oh immortal hoary almond:
Bare, yet in flower,
Save me from my body and its sins,
My torment and its relief.

The world's misfortune and mine
I hold within my hand,
Oh flesh of urination, active and evil,
You who, making me, are good.

This is clearly not a very good poem; but it is typical (even in its quality) of a certain phase in Hernández's work, illustrating several themes and symbols important in the first period. The final stanza with its open reference to masturbation is not uncommonly frank; one finds a number of less abashed poems about genitals in this work. Such overtly genital sexuality fades with maturity, so that several of the symbols associated with it—figs, snakes, and lemons—do not endure beyond this stage.[30]

The snake image is the most interesting of the sexual symbols, because it undergoes a marked evolution within the span of the first period. From a simple equivalent to the phallus (see "Adolescent," p. 36; "The Adolescent," p. 41; XVI and XL of *Expert*), the snake comes to represent the undirected and self-destructive lust of the young man, especially in the poems "Bloody Fate" and "My Blood Is a Road" (see below, pp. 64–69). In "Sonreídme" ("Smile at Me," pp. 258–60), a poem which belongs (as do the two poems cited above) to the group we have labeled transitional, the snake represents another sort of force destructive of the young ego: religion, specifically the Catholic Church. Miguel exults over his liberation from this monster in a poem whose paratactic structure is reminiscent of the Bible or of a litany:

Vengo muy satisfecho de librarme
de la serpiente de las múltiples cúpulas,
la serpiente escamada de casullas y cálices;
su cola puso en mi boca acíbar, sus anillos verdugos
reprimieron y malaventuraron la nudosa sangre de mi corazón. (p. 258)

I am very satisfied that I have freed myself
From the serpent of the multiple cupolas,
The serpent scaled in chasubles and chalices;
Its tail filled my mouth with bitterness, its executioner rings
Repressed and brought grief to the knotty blood of my heart.

Such symbols as the countryside qua nurturing womb, the circle or wheel (self-contained and uroboric), and in fact the uroboric motif in general, appear only in this early work. "Come here to the country, sons of the furrow. Your life is the earth's as is your death. . . . [City people] have weaned you away from the countryside," Miguel writes in "Momento—*campesino*" ("Moment—*Rural*," p. 939), clearly describing the earth as nurturer and as uroboric container of opposites (death and life, in this instance). Again in "Oda—*al vino*" ("Ode—*To Wine*," pp. 83–85) he speaks of the earth as bountiful supplier and as unending, unchanging uroboros:

India del grano, asociación del lujo,
vinícola paisaje,
como un mediterráneo sin reflujo,
ni flujo ni oleaje,
sólo esplendor y espuma de ramaje. (pp. 83–84)

Wealth of grapes, society of profusion,
A vintager's landscape
Like a Mediterranean without ebb
Or flow or rush of waves,
Simply splendor and the spume of branches.

Miguel used the image of the uroboros frequently during his religious period. It refers to the Virgin Mary, "Justo anillo su vientre de Lo Justo" ("Perfect circlet her womb of the Perfect," p. 141), as well as to God, whom he calls "el Perfecto Anillo" ("the Perfect Ring," p. 441). The sea, like the snake eating its own tail, never dies except to be reborn, never ends, never begins. It is in fact another representation of the uroboros, as we can see in many of Hernández's poems.[31] In "Mar y Dios" ("Sea and God," p. 149) the poet compares God (a difficult, abstract notion) to the sea (a tangible, although complex, reality). Both are endless, both contain beginning and end, existence and death:

Elevando sus nadas hasta el bulto,
creando y descubriendo vas presencias,
y llevas las presentes a lo oculto.

Inexistencias paren existencias,
se cela en lo secreto lo patente,
nacen, mueren, sigilos, evidencias.
. . . .
Ni principio ni fin te halla la nave.
. . . .
y tú, tu resultado y tu problema,
eres tu concepción y nacimiento.

Elevating its nothings to form
You proceed to create and discover presences,
And you carry the present down to the hidden.

The nonexistent spawns the existent,
The patent is secreted in the hidden,
Concealment, manifestation are born and die.
. . . .
The ship finds neither beginning or end of you.
. . . .
You, your own solution and your problem,
You are your conception and birth.

The cicada and the crow are associated with the theme of transitoriness: the crow is a harbinger of death, and the cicada a creature doomed to die after one short season. The symbol of the cicada is fully developed in a poem which was probably written a little after *Expert in Moons,* "Cigarra—*excesiva*" ("Cicada—*Excessive*," pp. 91–92).[32] It is a poem typical of that period in that it is little more than a string of metaphors describing a given phenomenon. There are twenty-eight metaphors for the cicada in the fifty-five lines of the poem, based either on the insect's noisiness or its association with summer, the summer sun, or its ephemeral nature. Its identification with noise and with sun makes the cicada pre–eminently a male figure; its maleness in conjunction with its transitoriness make it a symbol for the adolescent male. Like the adolescent, it is shown to be self-destructive, incited by its own uncontrollable urges to a form of suicide. Miguel explicitly identifies himself with this insect when in the ninth stanza he begins to write in the first person.

A few of the metaphors referring to the transitory nature of the cicada are:

> Somnambulist of the sun, which guides his life
> Until death explodes

> Fate of the light, destiny of the skyrocket

> Brief swan of rage and asbestos who—what intoxication!—
> Fails to see that his song is the requiem for his death

> Trembling, burning from too much music,
> A brilliance which disturbs and burns.
> Dying such a burning living death,
> I, my best poem,
> Feeling its convulsion within my fingertip

Hernández emphasizes its solar nature in calling it "light," "product of the summer solstice," "prometheus of August," "tongue and fluttering wings / Of the most divine fire," "flame"; and its noise-making: "word," "musical dance," "falsetto nightingale," "fountain's beat," "pulse or heart." Some metaphors combine the two characteristics: "as much a turtledove of the sun as a siren," "baritone ignition of noonday," "skyrocket," "motor of summer," "language of the sun, Holy Spirit of the sun, dove of the sun."

The crow is seen in various poems as the omen of death. In "My Blood Is a Road" the poet implores the woman (to whom the poem is addressed) to satisfy him sexually, to

> Guárdame de sus sombras que graznan fatalmente
> girando en torno mío a picotazos,
> girasoles de cuervos borrascosos. (p. 239)

> Save me from the shadows which caw fatefully
> Wheeling about me and pecking,
> [Shadows of] stormy crows like so many sunflowers.

XI *Analysis of Representative Works*

Given the limitations of space which preclude full analyses of even a score of Hernández's best works in each period, I have opted to analyze in depth one of the prose works, the play, and several key poems. Of the prose works "Pozo—*vivo*" ("The Well—*Alive*," pp. 949–50) is, perhaps, the most typical. Like many of these pieces, it describes Hernández's immediate environment and is at the same time autobiographical. It recounts the early summer ritual of cleaning out the well, into which he is lowered by a rope, "hanged in comfort, purposely a bucket." The mythic undertones of the activity—the perilous descent into the maws of the earth, the reimmersion into the great wet darkness—are not lost on Hernández, for he calls himself a Christ, perceiving the similarity of his descent and Christ's entombment. To heighten the suspense and sense of danger surrounding his mission, Hernández develops a series of hypothetical mischances, all beginning with "if" followed by the past subjunctive: "if my sister were to close over the opening, were to make it impossible for me to see sky and daylight" (the feminine figure is clearly malevolent); "if this terrestrial skyscraper should collapse," "if the enormous resultant ring were to disintegrate," then "I would sample the darkness of my grave," "I would save the gravediggers some work," and "I would remain here in this water-cellar, ruined, pouring forth blood and water, christlike, from my side."

The archetypal identity of the well should be equally clear: it is wet, a "warehouse of water," a spring which constantly renews itself, "filling with nascent water the hole I leave in the already born [water]," filling it with "new water, suckling water, of unstoppable speed." And it is round, a fact which Hernández reiterates in a variety of ingenious ways in nearly every paragraph. The form of "The Well—*Alive*" is circular as well: it begins "In the summer . . . one day" and ends "at night. . . . In the autumn." He descends during the day and "ascends to the late afternoon." In style this piece typifies the first phase of Hernández's work. The vocabulary and syntax (especially the hyperbaton) combine to make it difficult to understand on a first reading: there is a lexicalized allusion (to Christ), a neologism ("tienta-tiempos," "weatherprober," for a thermometer), an extrapoetic word ("calzón de canto y tierra," "underdrawer of rock and earth"). The hyphenated title is also typical of this period, as Bruna Cinti points out. Paradoxically, it describes a "conjunction or whole, but, at the same time, a fracture."[33]

Carefully worked metaphors and ingenious images add to the density of the piece: "watched constantly by [my sister] from the curbstone of the mortal lens [i.e., not the well's lens]"; "In the autumn, the water comes up steaming in the upside-down bell that is the pail, like a tame bear pulled by a cord." The paragraphs (like the title) are structured around paradox ("Taking away the surface, I take away the depth"); antitheses (descent/ascent; heat above/coolness below; Miguel diminishing the spring replenishing its volume) or some other grammatical or lexical contrast (the if-then series previously elaborated; the goats and the lemon trees drink water which is sweeter because it is clean and fresher because it is new; in the goat pen there is a circular sky of zinc—presumably a zinc container full of water, reflecting the night sky—and in the garden another, terrestrial sky—seen from the perspective of the bottom of the well), which Cinti sees as characteristic of all of these prose poems.

While the piece is interesting as an example of Hernández's early style and subject matter, its greatest interest lies in its early depiction of a physical image which will assume great importance in Hernández's work: the image of the young man or vital force constrained, immured, enclosed. Some of the most desperate poems in *Thunderbolt* are built around this motif, which continues through the war years and into the last poems. The importance of this motif is underlined by Berns's study. He sees a strain of "forceful violence" in all of Hernández's work, a thematic violence often restrained structurally, physically, through the use of restrictive verse forms, through a careful choice of images (p. 21), or a mundane vocabulary

(p. 46), and a "constant framing of multiple perspectives" of reality (p. 60).

Other prose poems of this period treat such topics as a Sunday burial, Miguel's mute canary, March gardening, two local blind beggars, his stealing avocados with a gang of boys, thunder, and the she-goat ("formula of femininity"); some are purely descriptive, whereas others, like "The Well," have a figurative as well as literal level.

The only play we have included in this period is *How You've Changed! and A Shadow of Your Former Self.* Historically, the *auto sacramental* was a short allegorical play written to be performed at municipal celebrations of Corpus Christi. It generally dramatized some sacred story (Biblical, traditional, or hagiological). Under Calderón de la Barca (1600–1680) the *auto* reached its highest level of development; it began to fall from favor in the eighteenth century, and in 1765 Charles III prohibited further productions of the *auto*. "From that time onwards the *autos* were gradually forgotten and references to them become rare."[34] Hernández's revival of the *auto* was not entirely unprecedented (Rafael Alberti and Carlos de la Rica have each written one), but so unusual that it occasioned great interest in Madrid. Ramón Sijé undoubtedly encouraged Miguel in this revival, for, ever a proselytizer, he recognized the eminently didactic potential of the theater. "It is necessary to create a great theater for the majority . . . which will channel the energy they waste and clear up the doubts they have," he wrote (Ramos, p. 67). It is interesting to note that although Hernández disavowed the religious aims of Sijé in later years, he accepted and put into practice during the war years Sijé's belief that drama was the didactic medium *par excellence*.

Since Calderón's approximately seventy *autos sacramentales* effectively defined the genre, it is logical that anyone wishing to revive the genre would go to Calderón's *autos* for guidance. This Hernández certainly did, although there seem to be relatively few direct echoes of Calderón in this *auto*.[35]

The play has three Parts (each approximately as long as an entire Calderonian *auto*, i.e., about two thousand lines), corresponding to the three stages of Christian man: (1) Innocence; (2) Evil Passions; (3) Repentance. Cano Ballesta summarizes its stylistic features: "The *auto*—as is typical in Calderón—rests on a series of parallelistic correlations: five-membered for the five senses, four-membered when the four seasons or the four echoes appear. The image, the vocabulary, and the syntactic structure are clear exponents of the deep Calderonian and Baroque imprint" (p. 31). He also writes that the metric forms are the "traditional ones of the classic theater" (p. 31), but it should be pointed out that Calderón rarely used anything but an octosyllabic line in his *autos*, so that Hernández's incorporation into the *auto* of the great variety of forms found in the traditional *comedia* was in fact innovative.

In the first part of the play we are introduced to the Man-Child and his parents, the Husband and the Wife. The boy's days are spent playing with wild creatures and learning about the marvelous world around him. The Wife relates a dream she has had in which the Man-Child almost falls into a treacherous river. At the last moment he is rescued by "dos ángeles de pluma / y una vírgen de prisa" ("two angels in feathers / and a virgin in a hurry," p. 445, a typical Hernández play on words). The dream is a prefiguring of the nearly fatal moral fall the Man-Child will suffer, and of the supernatural intervention which will save him. Most of Part I details the encounters of Love and Innocence (old friends of the Man-Child) with Desire, her companion the Wind, and the Five Senses, who join forces with Desire to tempt the Man-Child to sin. He resists, but Flesh finally convinces him to eat of the apple. Immediately he loses his innocence and realizes that henceforth he will have to eat by the sweat of his brow and that, more appalling, he is the tangible result of his revered parents' lust.

In Part II the Man—no longer called the Man-Child—settles into his new life. The Four Seasons present themselves and he is allowed to choose one. Greedily he opts for Summer, but is soon made to realize that the farmer's work is unrelenting in the summer. When he collapses in exhaustion, a compassionate Shepherd descends from the hills to aid him. Revived, the Man rejects the Shepherd's invitation to follow him, although he envies the seemingly easier life. Desire incites him to kill the Shepherd, Flesh to take the Shepherd's wife. With the arrival of the Five Senses, the incitement takes on a political tone:

HEARING: The world belongs to everybody. . . .
FLESH: We are all equal. . . .
HEARING: Down with the exploiters!
SIGHT: Down with them, say I!

SMELL: The general strike! . . .
TOUCH: God is a myth!
FLESH: Religion is a moribund system of incense which perfumes corruption. (pp. 517–18)

The Man agrees to the deed. The two scenes preceding the murder—the first a lyrical interlude between the Shepherd and his wife and the second a conversation between Man and Desire (repeated with distortions by the Four Echoes, who represent the Man's conscience)—exemplify Hernández's originality within the conventional limits of this genre. The wife's lamentations over the Shepherd's body are repeated poignantly by the Four Echoes, whose role has been compared to that of the Greek chorus.

Part III finds the Man beginning to repent under the influence of the prophet Voice-of-Truth, a St. John preparing for the Lord's advent. Desire, Flesh, and the Five Senses assassinate this prophet, but his message has affected the Man. He dismisses Desire, who cries petulantly:

> But I will avenge myself
> On all. Vengeance! Yes!
> I will foment as soon as I can
> A social revolution.
> I'm going to the universities
> To tell all about this.
> . . . .
> The hammer and the sickle will be
> Your death and our motto; . . . (p. 557)

He then converts all of the Senses, who exclaim one by one, "How changed I am!". The Good Worker appears and invites the Man to follow him and work in his vineyard. They break bread together, whereupon the Worker's true identity as Christ is revealed. The last three scenes show Desire and a band of revolutionaries—armed with hammers and sickles—advancing to take revenge on the Man. Reassured by the Lord that he need not fear death, the Man dies at peace:

> A punto está la corrida:
> y en el momento de verte,
> toro negro, toro fuerte,
> estoy queriendo la vida
> y deseando la muerte. (p. 578)

> The bullfight is imminent:
> In the moment of seeing you,
> Black bull, strong bull,
> I am loving life
> And desiring my death.

This play has been criticized for its lack of drama (Ruíz Ramón, p. 310), for its "cold, slow schoolroom flavor" and the "sermonizing puppets" instead of characters (Puccini, pp. 29–30). In fact these criticisms are well grounded, although we should hardly expect to find well-developed characters in an allegory. The *auto* has its defenders, like Concha Zardoya, who finds certain scenes of the play "rigorously original, both as drama and as poetry, impregnated even then with that peculiar humanity and deep realism which all the later works exuded" (pp. 705–706). Bertini elaborates: "The whole *auto* . . . offers marks of authentic originality, above all because of its autobiographical background. Thus [the play] stands apart from the classical *autos sacramentales*, in which the author's personality is practically annulled in favor of the dogmatic message. Hernández has known how to structure the religious representation [at the same time] implanting in it his own life, the reality of his contacts with nature and of the vicissitudes of the shepherd's and farmer's lives" (p. 169).

How You've Changed!—does touch on many of the motifs and themes which characterize Hernández's later work: his conception of conjugal love, the almost sacral nature of procreation, exaltation of labor, and (from a point of view antithetical to his later one) social revolution.[36] Additionally, Parts I and II dramatize the psychological stage which Hernández was passing through in the first period of his work: in the beginning the Man-Child lives contentedly with his parents in the abundance of nature. With the incitement of Flesh and Desire—or adolescence—he is driven not only to rebel against them but to the edge of madness. Part II, the Stage of Evil Passions, shows the Man acceding repeatedly to Desire, taking the self-indulgent route rather than disciplining himself. The markedly sexual nature of his temptations shows this struggle to be Hernández's own, depicted so frequently in the verse of the period. Part III prefigures both the second and third periods of Hernández's work: the Man makes his own way in the world and is then able to face death with equanimity.

In short, Hernández's *auto sacramental* has some interesting features, both as regards his own personal development and as a revival of a forgotten genre. But it is overly didactic for modern taste, too long, and clumsily executed in its scenography. Hernández was to repudiate the play two years after he had written it, not because of its quality, but because he no longer believed in the dogma it dramatized: "Some time has passed since the publication of this work, and now I neither think nor feel many of the things I said in it. . . . I'm fed up and regretful about having done things in the service of God and that Catholic nonsense. . . . I was belying my earthly voice and nature utterly, I was betraying myself and killing myself pathetically" (from a letter to Juan Guerrero Ruíz, dated May 12, 1935, quoted in Ramos, p. 183).

XII   Analysis of Poems

It is clearly in the poetry of the first period that Hernández finds his own voice. For many, even had Hernández never written another line, the sonnets of *The Unending Thunderbolt* would have sufficed to give him a place among the greatest of Spanish poets. Most are agreed that *Expert in Moons*, while representing an astonishing personal achievement for a poor and minimally educated goatherd, is too hermetic, too dense and too impersonal to be more than a curiosity (standing beside *How You've Changed!*). Gerardo Diego (whose Gongorine poems in *Fábula de Equis y Zeda* are scarcely examples of lucidity) comments on the difficulty of the poems in *Expert*: "I do not believe that there is a single reader, or that there was one in 1933 either, capable of solving all the poetic riddles he proposes. Because they are riddles which only rarely and surreptitiously surrender, let slip, the solution. The riddle is a poetic genre as old as popular poetry, and the double or triple delight we take in the wit, the surprise, and the poetic emotion . . . comes together in a delicious synthesis."[37] It is not surprising then that these poems have only rarely been analyzed in the critical work on Hernández. The most complete analyses are those of Gabriel Berns of the poems IX and XXVIII (Diss., pp. 38–48; reprinted in *Hispanic Review*, 38 [1970], 388–93), and of Agustín Sánchez Vidal, "Un gongorismo personal (Algunas notas sobre *Perito en lunas*)," in Ifach's *Miguel Hernández*, pp. 184–200.

I have chosen one of the simpler octaves for analysis because of the difficulty of translating the multiple word plays in the denser ones:

XIV

Blanco narciso por obligación.
Frente a su imagen siempre, espumas pinta,
y en el mineral lado del salón
una idea de mar fulge distinta.
Si no esquileo en campo de jabón,
hace rayas, con gracia, mas sin tinta;
y al fin, con el pulgar en ejercicio,
lo que le sobra anula del oficio. (p. 65)

White narcissus by obligation.
Always facing his own image, he paints foam,
And on the mineral side of the salon,
There shines distinctly an idea of the sea.
If he doesn't shear in fields of soap,
He does draw lines, with grace, but without ink;
And finally, with his thumb performing a drill
He obliterates the excesses of his office.

When published, the poem was untitled and far more difficult to decipher (Zardoya conjectured that the "white narcissus" was the moon, p. 650) than after Cano Ballesta published the octaves' titles. This one is "Barber," and the ingenious metaphors which compose the poem refer to the fact that the barber's job obliges him to wear white and stare into a mirror all day; he paints on lather (foam, fields of soap) which he doesn't shear but rather draws lines through (with the razor, not with ink, and gracefully); finally he wipes away any extra lather with his thumb. The "mineral side of the shop" is that part which is reflected in the mirror; the "idea of the sea" is probably a mirror image of the basin of water. Hernández calls it an "idea" of the sea because it is not the real sea, but a reflection of it. (The basin of water is not precisely the sea either, of course.) In Platonic terms, the mirror image and the poet's description of it are reproductions of an object which is itself a replica of its Ideal.

The poem is an *octava real*, eight hendecasyllabic verses stressed on the sixth and tenth syllables. This fixed internal stress only twice falls on and thus reinforces important words: verses 4 ("mar," sea) and 6 ("-gar," the second syllable of "pulgar," thumb, and so not strictly a word in itself, but an important sound, harsh and dissonant in the context of the otherwise smooth line. It is a sudden violent intrusion, which might be forgotten were it not for the military "en

ejercicio," drilling, and the euphemistically threatening tone of the
last verse.). The other stressed syllables have been chosen, it would
appear, for alliterative effect: the *o* in "por" (verse 1) is echoed four
times in the verse; the "siem-" of verse 2 with its *s* and *m* accen-
tuates the *s*'s and the nasal *m*'s and *n*'s which abound in the verse;
the "la" of verse 3 provides one of five *l*'s in the verse, etc. The tenth
syllables of the body of the octave, excluding the rhymed couplet at
the end, are notable in that all end in *n*. The poem's diction is rather
straightforward in comparison to many in this collection. Several
words stand out: "narcissus," an allusion, and a proper name ren-
dered generic; "salon," a Gallicism as inappropriate in Spanish to
signify a "barbershop" as it would be in English (obviously chosen to
fit the rhyme scheme); "esquileo," or sheep-shearing, which Guerrero Zamora points out as a regional word (p. 204). The only example of hyperbaton is the last verse, although verses 5 and 6 invert
one of Góngora's favorite lexical formulas—"A, si no B" ("A, if not
B")—which is a kind of disruption in an expected word order.

"Barber" exemplifies both what the critics have found praiseworthy and blameworthy in *Expert in Moons*. Guerrero Zamora summarizes these feelings: "He totally masters the hendecasyllable, but
he convolutes it to the point of irritation. Moreover, he has overcome the resistance of rhyme. . . . With so much effort, yes, he has
won the game of form, but he has lost the game of emotion" (p. 214).
"Barber" is interesting, a clever composition, but like most of the
octaves in *Expert*, it is cold and forgettable. Zardoya defends the
work against such criticism: "Not one critic has noticed the human
drama there is in this book. If they had seen the house he grew up
in, they would have understood this, his first reaction against the
dung which surrounded him" (p. 647). Yet in the end, our critical
reaction to a book must be based on that book, not on the circumstances from which it grew.

The Unending Thunderbolt is the book which identified Hernández as one of the great poetic voices in pre–Civil War Spain, so full
of brilliant poets. Juan Ramón wrote: "All the friends of 'pure
poetry' should seek out and read these vibrant poems. Their wrap-
ping reminds us of Quevedo, it is true, of his pure heritage. But the
rough, tremendous beauty of [Hernández's] deep-rooted heart
bursts the package and overflows, like elementary, naked nature"
(quoted in Cano Ballesta, p. 43). The book was in fact anything but
"elementary, naked nature"; it was a meticulously organized,
painstakingly revised collection which had occupied Miguel for

nearly two years. Dario Puccini has an excellent analysis of the changes Hernández made in the successive versions of this book, beginning with the tentative formulation of *The Image of Your Footprint*, through *The Grievéd Whistling* to the definitive *Thunderbolt* (pp. 42–55). He believes that the changes reflect Miguel's maturing vision of the world as well as his increasing poetic skills. The thematic emphasis of the first version, according to Puccini, is the "private discourse of love"; of the second, the poet's "cry of anguish" (p. 44); and of *Thunderbolt*, a sense of tragedy, "solemn and bitter . . . which seems to blossom forth from some abysmal depth of total, corporeal, age-old anguish" (p. 49).

There are twenty-seven sonnets and three longer poems in *Thunderbolt*, distributed symmetrically: one long poem "Un carnívoro cuchillo" ("A Carnivorous Knife"); thirteen sonnets; another long poem ("I Call Myself Mud . . ."); thirteen sonnets; another long poem (the "Elegy to Ramón Sijé"); and one final sonnet. This pattern, as Manuel Ruíz Funes points out in his monograph on *Thunderbolt*, indicates "that the author is aware . . . that a book of poetry should have a rhythm, external as it were, corresponding to the metrical rhythm."[38] Arturo Pérez identifies a "premeditated dramatic structure" in the arrangement of the poems, beginning with "(a) Statement of the problem: love and jealousy (sonnet 14). (b) Presentiment of death in love (sonnet 17). (c) Forces in conflict: bull-bullfighter, love-moral code (sonnet 23). (d) Final tragic outcome: weeping (sonnet 26); death (sonnet 28)."[39]

From the first hallucinatory vision of the carnivorous knife hovering about Hernández's life to the peculiar "Final Sonnet" (peculiar because its Baroque diction and melancholy, no longer anguished, tone make it seem radically out of place, otherworldly, coming as it does immediately after the desperate and very modern elegy for Sijé), *The Unending Thunderbolt* records Hernández's difficult path to self-discovery. Love, the emotion which drives one to experience the fullest range of feelings, is an ideal stimulus and starting point for such an exploration. From his experience with love, Hernández learns a variety of other facts about himself: he is stubborn, he is iconoclastic, he seems fated to suffering, he is too generous of himself, he will die. Death is the corollary of pain; both result from an imperfection in the system. Puccini sees love's role in *Thunderbolt* as that of "a hidden duty . . . or the energy which manages to dramatize his heart to the fullest, to represent tragically his adverse luck, to exalt his bloody and rebellious vehemence" (p. 49). Thus

The Unending Thunderbolt is not precisely love poetry in the traditional sense, although love was its cause:

> Al doloroso trato de la espina,
> al fatal desaliento de la rosa
> y a la acción corrosiva de la muerte
>
> arrojado me veo, y tanta ruina
> no es por otra desgracia ni otra cosa
> que por quererte y sólo por quererte.
> (p. 231)

> To the painful treatment of the thorn,
> To the fatal discouragement of the rose
> And to the corrosive action of death
>
> I see myself thrown, and all this ruin
> Befalls not for any other cause or reason
> Than for loving you; simply for loving you.

Clearly, the pain of love suffuses the poetry:

> Umbrío por la pena, casi bruno,
> porque la pena tizna cuando estalla,
> donde yo no me hallo no se halla
> hombre más apenado que ninguno.
>
> Sobre la pena duermo solo y uno,
> pena es mi paz y pena mi batalla, . . . (p. 216)

> Umber from the pain, nearly black,
> Because pain soots when it explodes,
> Where I am not, there is not
> The most tormented man alive.
>
> I sleep on the pain solitary and single,
> Pain is my peace and pain my battle, . . .

> Tengo estos huesos hechos a las penas
> y a las cavilaciones estas sienes:
> pena que vas, cavilación que vienes
> como el mar de la playa a las arenas. (p. 218)

I have accustomed these bones to grief
And these temples to suspicion:
Grief goes, suspicion comes
Like the sea from the beach to the sand.

Si la sangre también, como el cabello,
con el dolor y el tiempo encaneciera,
mi sangre, roja hasta el carbunclo, fuera
pálida hasta el temor y hasta el destello. (p. 222)

If blood too, like hair,
Grew white with sorrows and time
My blood, red as a garnet, would be
pale as fear, pale as a beam.

And the frustration of his physical love is apparent (see also sonnets 4, 11, 25):

No me conformo, no: me desespero
como si fuera un huracán de lava
en el presidio de una almendra esclava
o en el penal colgante de un jilguero.

Besarte fue besar un avispero
que me clava al tormento y me desclava
y cava un hoyo fúnebre y lo cava
dentro del corazón donde me muero. (p. 224)

I do not resign myself, no: I despair
As if I were a hurricane of lava
In the penitentiary of an almond enslaved
Or in the hanging prison of a linnet.

Kissing you was kissing a wasp's nest
Which nails me to the rack and frees me
And digs a gloomy grave and digs it
Inside my heart where I am dying.

XIII *The Title Poem, "El rayo que no cesa"*

In spite of this omnipresence of love, *The Unending Thunderbolt* is not in the final analysis a collection of love poetry, for its focus is on the poet, not on his beloved. The poem which Hernández must have judged the key to the work is the first sonnet, not only because of its position but because he drew the title of the book from it. We shall analyze it at some length.

¿No cesará este rayo que me habita
el corazón de exasperadas fieras
y de fraguas coléricas y herreras
donde el metal más fresco se marchita?

¿No cesará esta terca estalactita
de cultivar sus duras caballeras
como espadas y rígidas hogueras
hacia mi corazón que muge y grita?

Este rayo ni cesa ni se agota:
de mí mismo tomó su procedencia
y ejercita en mí mismo sus furores.

Esta obstinada piedra de mí brota
y sobre mí dirige la insistencia
de sus lluviosos rayos destructores.

Will it not cease, this lightning flash which inhabits
My heart with exasperated beasts
And furious forges and blacksmiths' wives
Where the freshest metal withers?

Will it not cease, this stubborn stalactite,
Cultivating its stiff switches of hair
Like swords and rigid bonfires
Toward my heart which bellows and cries out?

This lightning neither ceases nor runs dry;
It was from me alone that it sprang
And on me alone it trains its rages.

This obstinate rock sprouts from me
And it turns on me the insistence
Of its rainy and destructive bolts.

"Will it not cease . . ." is one of seventy classical sonnets written during the first period. The "classical" sonnet in Spanish is the hendecasyllabic, with identical rhyme schemes in the quatrains (*abba, abba,*), varied in the tercets (although Hernández uses *cde, cde* in all of the sonnets of *Thunderbolt*). All of the verses except the second—which is accented on the fourth, eighth, and tenth syllables—are accented on the sixth and tenth syllables. Since it constitutes a break in the pattern, verse 2 receives special emphasis. Its stuttering rhythm gives the line a pathetic tone, as though the speaker's voice had broken. The organization of the sonnet is simple and precise: the first quatrain poses a question, the second rephrases it. The tercets answer the questions, and do so emphatically. The doubly negative neither-nor construction of the first tercet precludes any appeal. The second tercet is an unequivocal statement of fact.

In contrast to its classical form, the vocabulary and syntax of the poem are modern. There are no neologisms, no abstruse words, no hyperbaton. In their place, we find a vocabulary drawn from nature, yet not at all natural, for the words are combined in bizarre ways: unlike objects are lumped together—forges and beasts and blacksmiths' wives; stalactites, hearts, and swords—and unlikely modifiers make mundane objects seem fantastic: thunderbolts living in hearts, exasperated beasts, furious forges, stubborn stalactites with stiff switches of hair, obstinate rocks which emit lightning. A study of the vocabulary of this poem shades inevitably into a study of its figurative language, for through his combinations of words Hernández creates what Carlos Bousoño has called "visions" (see above, pp. 32–33), a sort of surrealistic metaphor.

Yet Hernández has not abandoned traditional metaphors and similes—the poem is rich with them. And he is in control of them, as he was not in *Expert*, where they became the whole poem. Hernández uses the metaphors to describe (a) that which causes him anguish and (b) that part of himself—the "heart"—affected. Judging from many of the poems in *Thunderbolt*, we might conjecture that the reason for his pain is frustration in love. But that is inexact, just as it is inexact to label the book "love poetry." The cause of his grief is described in an abstract, detached way. Moreover, there is no second person pronoun. We must look deeper.

The agents-of-pain are a lightning bolt, described and developed in the first quatrain and tercet, and a stalactite, developed in the second quatrain and tercet. While the appearance of the lightning is not mentioned, that of the stalactite is the basis for several metaphors. It has "stiff switches of hair / like swords and rigid bonfires," and it is an "obstinate rock" which hurls murderous and rainy thunderbolts. The "rigid bonfire" suggests petrified flames, whose shape would be similar (if inverted) to a stalactite's or to a lightning bolt's. Another image which refers both to the lightning and to the stalactite is that of the "rainy thunderbolt." It makes us think of lightning flashing in the rain, or of a stalactite which resembles a wet fork of lightning, petrified. Hernández took care, then, to emphasize the similarities of these two dominant images. Both are "piercing" in Ávila's terminology, or phallic, and both are associated with water. They are also deadly. These characteristics immediately suggest the destructive sexual urges of the young man, aroused by some avatar of the Great Mother. (Several other poems in *Thunderbolt* use the image of the lightning flash to represent the same sexually inspired, irresistible urge to annihilation, precariously contained: "una revolución dentro de un hueso, / un rayo soy sujeto a una redoma," "I am a revolution [immured] in a bone, / A thunderbolt contained in a flask," p. 224.)

But there is more to this poem than the solar/chthonic theme: we also see Hernández's growing perception that he is fated to suffer. This realization by the emerging ego that his fate is not generic but personal is one of the prevalent themes of the latter part of the first period. Hernández underlines the point by almost monotonous reiteration of a first person pronoun, which appears six times, twice with the intensifying (both in sound and meaning) "mismo" (which is literally translated "myself," although I have changed it to "alone"). "Will it not cease?" he asks himself incredulously, and then answers reluctantly, "No." The immediate stimulus of his suffering may change—and it did—but he recognizes in himself an uncompromising nature which will inevitably lead him to take difficult—often painful—positions. Herrero speaks of this aspect of his character when he writes: "That awareness of risking death, of the possible catastrophic consequences of his generous surrender to life and to others is constant in Hernández and constitutes one of his most characteristic traits" (p. 149).

The stalactite and the lightning bolt may be likened on the basis of shape (although it took a vivid imagination to do so), but the differences between the two, although unmentioned in the poem, are also significant. Principally, there is a difference in their formation, for the bolt is created instantaneously, the stalactite very slowly; and in their duration: the lightning lasts a moment, the stalactite forever. By choosing these two objects to represent the cause of his pain, Hernández suggests that the pain has all the immediacy, the intensity of a thunderbolt, coupled with the perdurability of the stalactite; that the pain seems to be born anew each moment and yet have the force of centuries behind it.

The second group of metaphors in "Will it not cease . . ." refers to the poet's heart or spirit, wounded by his cruel fate. It is a heart full of "exasperated beasts," of "furious forges and blacksmiths' wives" where the freshest or coolest metal crumples. His heart "bellows and cries out," as well it might since it is inhabited by beasts. Animals of all sorts figure in the mythology of the Great Mother; sometimes they are seen as her henchmen, sometimes as the objectified inner passions of the young man, which render him beastlike (compare especially "Me llamo carro, "I Call Myself Mud . . ."). The image of the forge, especially when combined with that of lightning, provides an example of indirect allusion, for it calls to mind Vulcan at his forge, making thunderbolts for the gods. The forge is associated with light, heat, and fire—as are lightning bolts—and is thus symbolic of the destructive masculinity which destroys the youth, the "freshest metal." It is appropriate that this forge be filled with women (blacksmiths' wives or female blacksmiths, since the word is ambiguous in Spanish).

The pattern of sound in the poem tends to reinforce the visual imagery. Hernández used stops (sounds whose pronunciation requires a full obstruction of air: /p, t, k, b, d, g, č /) and fricatives (sounds produced by forcing the breath through a constricted passage: /f, s, x, ∅ or th/) abundantly, the stops perhaps to imitate the claps of thunder which accompany lightning as well as the crash of metal being beaten on a forge. They may suggest as well the regular drip/stop process which builds up a stalactite. The fricatives may suggest the hissing of those rainy forks of lightning, as well as the sound of newly forged metal being plunged into water.

XIV   *"Como el Toro"*

I should like quite briefly to analyze one other poem—probably the best known—of *The Unending Thunderbolt*. It is a standard anthology piece, as it deserves to be; the first line has become one of Hernández's most famous.

Como el toro he nacido para el luto
y el dolor, como el toro estoy marcado
por un hierro infernal en el costado
y por varón en la ingle con un fruto.

Como el toro lo encuentra diminuto
todo mi corazón desmesurado,
y del rostro del beso enamorado,
como el toro a tu amor se lo disputo.

Como el toro me crezco en el castigo,
la lengua en corazón tengo bañada
y llevo al cuello un vendaval sonoro.

Como el toro te sigo y te persigo,
y dejas mi deseo en una espada,
como el toro burlado, como el toro. (p. 226)

Like the bull I was born for mourning
And for pain, like the bull I am branded
By an infernal iron in the flank
And as a male in the groin with a fruit.

Like the bull my intemperate heart
Finds everything diminutive,
And enamored by the face's kiss
Like the bull I fight your love for it.

Like the bull I grow in punishment,
I have a tongue drenched in heart
And around my neck I carry a sonorous tempest.

Like the bull I sue you and pursue you,
And you leave my desire on a sword,
Like the bull deceived, like the bull.

The principal reason for the popularity of this poem—for it is a fine poem, but no more so than many others in *Thunderbolt*—lies in its clear development of the analogies between Miguel and the bull, analogies which later critics have amplified and sanctified. Cano Ballesta, for instance, writes that Hernández's symbolic use of the bull "sums up in itself all the essential aspects of his world view" (p. 94), that it is "the distillate of and key to his poetic world" (p. 96).

We must disagree with the sweeping nature of this affirmation, for the bull appears with frequency only in the first period (Hernández was an *aficionado* as a boy, and during his second stay in Madrid he was employed writing a taurine encyclopedia), less frequently in the second period (as a symbol of the aggressively masculine Republicans, in contrast to the Nationalists who are oxen, or castrated bulls), and not at all in the third. Since the bull is a traditional figure in the Great Mother archetype—"the male instrument of fertility and also its victim . . . the bull symbolizes the youthful god, son-lover of the Great Mother" (Neumann, *Origins*, p. 22)—it is not surprising that we find it limited essentially to this early work.[40]

Cano Ballesta has enumerated (pp. 96–99) the parallels Hernández describes between himself and the bull in this poem: (1) both are destined to pain and mourning; (2) both are marked as males by their external genitalia; (3) their immoderate hearts (I believe this is a misreading of the poem: Hernández compares his heart not to the bull's heart, but to the bull himself, for both find the world too small); (4) their indomitable bravery, growing in punishment; (5) "sincere externalization of his interiority," the bull gushing blood and lowing, Miguel doing the same in his verse; (6) perseverance, pursuing the objects of their desire stubbornly; (7) the tragic destiny of both (the bull's tragic fate "is decisive in [Miguel's] choice of him as a symbol").

Hernández has used a variety of structuring devices which interlock to leave no "loose ends" in the poem: all elements are paired or grouped with others. This reflects Hernández's argument that he and the bull are "paired" by fate, that he and his beloved are tied by love but rent by differing morals, and so forth. (It is also an early example of his belief that the nature of life is bipolar or antithetical, a belief nurtured by the somewhat simplistic value judgments he espoused during the war years, and coming into flower during his last years.[41]) The "bimembrations" and "parallelisms" are also reflections of continuing Golden Age influence on his work. I shall point out a few of these structural recourses:

1. The first two verses are an example of chiasmus (an inversion of the second of two parallel structures, *AB—BA*. In this case *A* is a verbal phrase beginning with "Like the bull . . .").

2. Verses 3 and 4 begin with what appear to be parallel prepositional phrases but are not. Hernández has tricked us here. The true parallel to "by an iron" is "with a fruit."

3. Stanza 2 is framed—begun and ended—with verses whose first segment is identical ("Like the bull") and whose second is parallel.

4. The first tercet is tripartite, with each verse describing a point of similarity between the bull and the poet. Since it is a comparison of two objects, it is also binary.

5. The final tercet begins and ends with "like the bull," as does the final verse.

Interstrophic (stanza-by-stanza) development is also important: in the first quatrain Hernández sets forth the two principal similarities between himself and the bull: both are destined to suffer, both are male (the brand on Hernández's flank or side may refer to the Biblical tradition whereby Adam lost a rib to make Eve). The second quatrain details what impels the two of them into the ring (or fatal struggle with life): in general, they find the world too small to accommodate them and seek to conquer new territory; specifically, Hernández wishes to wrest a kiss from his beloved. The first tercet describes them in the ring: both grow angrier and larger (on another level this is undoubtedly a sexual reference) with excitement; the bull physical gushing of blood parallels Hernández's lyrical outpourings, as his sonorous and anguished bellowing does Hernández's writings. The outcome of the bull's pursuit of the cape and Hernández's of his woman is the same: both are impaled (the archetypal reference here is clear: sexual passion, objectified in the sword, is his enemy); both are tricked, disappointed, frustrated, ridiculed ("burlado" has all of these connotations in Spanish).

XV   "*Mi sangre es un camino*"

Before finishing with the first period in Hernández's work I should like to analyze a part of one of the transitional poems (the length of these poems precludes a full analysis here): "Mi sangre es un camino" "My Blood Is a Road"; pp. 237–39). It is one of a dozen poems which I have labeled transitional because while the themes are typical of the first period, the style is that of the second. This particular poem is similar to two other major poems of this period: "I call myself mud . . ." which in spite of its placement in the heart of *Thunderbolt* was composed later than most of the sonnets; and "Sino sangriento" ("Bloody Fate"), The more classically structured and restrained "A Carnivorous Knife" is also similar to "My Blood Is a Road."

Me empuja a martillazos y a mordiscos,
me tira con bramidos y cordeles
del corazón, del pie, de los orígenes,
. . . .
Mujer, mira una sangre,
mira una blusa de azafrán en celo,
mira un capote líquido ciñéndose en mis huesos
como descomunales serpientes que me oprimen
acarreando angustia por mis venas.

Mira una fuente alzada de amorosos collares
y cencerros de voz atribulada
temblando de impaciencia por ocupar tu cuello,
un dictamen feroz, una sentencia,
una exigencia, una dolencia, un río . . . .
. . . .
Mírala con sus chivos y sus toros suicidas
corneando cabestros y montañas,
. . . .
La puerta de mi sangre está en la esquina
del hacha y de la piedra,
pero en ti está la entrada irremediable.

Necesito extender este imperioso reino,
prolongar a mis padres hasta la eternidad,
y tiendo hacia ti un puente de arqueados corazones
que ya se corrompieron y que aún laten.

No me pongas obstáculos que tengo que salvar,
no me siembres de cárceles,
no bastan cerraduras ni cementos,
no, a encadenar mi sangre de alquitrán inflamado . . . .
. . . .
¡Ay qué ganas de amarte contra un árbol,
ay qué afán de trillarte en una era,
. . . .
Mi sangre es un camino ante el crepúsculo
de apasionado barro y charcos vaporosos
que tiene que acabar en tus entrañas,
un depósito mágico de anillos
que ajustar a tu sangre,
. . . .
Recibe esta fortuna sedienta de tu boca
que para ti heredé de tanto padre. (pp. 237–39)

It prods me with hammer blows and bites,
It pulls me with roars and cords
By the heart, by the foot, by my origins,

Woman, behold a blood,
Behold a blouse of rutting saffron stigmas,
Behold a liquid cape girding itself in my bones
Like monstrous serpents which squeeze me
Bearing anguish through my veins.

Behold an upraised fountain of loving necklaces
And cowbells of plaintive voice
Trembling with impatience to occupy your neck,
A fierce dictate, a sentence,
A demand, an ache, a river . . . .
. . . .
Behold it with its he-goats and suicidal bulls
Seeking death from head to tail,
. . . .
The door to my blood is on the corner
Between the axe and the rock,
But in you lies the irremediable entry.

I must extend this imperious reign,
Prolong my fathers until eternity,
And I stretch out toward you a bridge of retching hearts
Which are already decayed and which still beat.

Don't throw up any obstacles for me to clear,
Don't sow my way with prisons,
Neither locks nor cement are enough,
No, to shackle this blood like burning pitch . . . .
. . . .
Oh how I burn to love you against a tree,
How eagerly I would thresh you,
. . . .
My blood is a road before the twilight
Of impassioned mud and steamy puddles
Which must end in you,
A magical deposit of rings
To adjust to your blood,
. . . .
Receive this fortune thirsting for your mouth
Which I inherited for you from so many ancestors.

The poem is typical of the transitional group in its length and in its versification, which is a free grouping of seven-, eleven-, and fourteen-syllable lines. Hernández was experimenting during this phase with longer lines and new combinations of verses (two other combinations he tried were eleven- and seven-syllable lines and eleven- and fourteen-syllable lines), but the result was not precisely "free verse," as some critics have suggested (see Puccini, p. 64; Cano Ballesta, p. 293; Zardoya, p. 665) because the lines are always of traditional lengths. Moreover, the free combination of different verse lengths (with no fixed stanzas) is common in two classical Spanish verse forms, the *silva* and the *canción*. Neruda and Aleixandre, Hernández's mentors at the time he was writing these poems, did write free verse, with thoroughly irregular, unprecedented verse lengths.

The influence of Neruda[42] is evident in many other aspects of this poem. The vocabulary is impetuous, brutal, primitive, chaotic, Surrealistic: Nerudian, in a word. "Impure poetry" was the Chilean's goal, a poetry which might deal, he wrote, with "the decrees of touch, smell, taste, sight, hearing, the desire for justice, sexual desire, the noise of the ocean, without deliberately excluding anything, without deliberately accepting anything . . . " (cited in Cano Ballesta, p. 283). "My Blood Is a Road" seems to exemplify this willingness to consider any object or any experience as worthy of poetic treatment. The subject of the poem may be said to be Hernández's sexual desire; its aim is to convince a woman to satisfy that desire. The torrent of brutal and lascivious images which he paints for her seem better calculated to horrify than persuade.

There is also evidence of Neruda's influence in the syntax of the poem: the chaotic structure, numerous gerunds, frequent enumeration, and stylistic quirks such as the coordination of dissimilar, unparallel words ("roars and cords," "by the heart, by the foot, by my origins"). Moreover, the division of the poem into verses parallels Neruda's use of versicles, which Amado Alonso defines in his *Poesía y estilo de Pablo Neruda* (3rd ed., Buenos Aires: Editorial Sudamericana, 1966) as "a succession of free verses [corresponding] to a succession of intuitional units or else a special enjambment of intuitions, required by the movement of the sentimental effusion. Each verse sets apart, then, an intuitional unit, or, if not, it is linked with the preceding and the following ones . . . " (p. 88). Hernández relied more heavily on enjambment than Neruda because he was still using verses of fixed length. Each stanza in "My Blood Is a Road" is a syntactical-logical unity: except for the final two, each stanza is one complete (albeit complex) sentence.

This poem is similar to much of Hernández's earlier work in that it consists of groups of metaphors and similes. Now, however, not all of the metaphors describe objects. Many attempt to describe feelings: sexual desires, procreative wishes, fear of rejection and extinction; or intuitions about himself: he is destined to be the thrall of his passions, that is, his blood is a road, a foreordained path through life. There are metaphors which transmute objects, too: his phallus is "a blouse of rutting saffron," swollen with a "liquid cape" of blood; it is an "upraised fountain" of necklaces to "occupy" her neck. Semen is described as a "bridge of retching hearts," a "magical deposit of rings" (and with several other images we have not translated for brevity's sake).

Hernández begins in this poem to exploit what Philip Wheelwright calls the "diaphoric" nature of metaphor, in which the mere juxtaposition of diverse elements creates new meanings; heretofore he had used "epiphor" (the traditional use of metaphor) to express a similarity between something already well known (the vehicle) and something which is less well known (the tenor).[43] Epiphor still predominates in this poem, but it is important to note the introduction of the diaphoric element, for it will become increasingly important in later periods. An example of diaphor, in which purely by the juxtaposition of elements Hernández likens the woman to a cow and himself to a bull eager to mount her:

> Behold an upraised fountain of loving necklaces
> And cowbells of plaintive voice
> Trembling with impatience to occupy your neck.

It is not until several verses later that Hernández explicitly mentions bulls.

The overall structure of the poem becomes clear after several readings. All of the stanzas up until the shortest in the poem, the one that begins "The door to my blood," describe the physical effects of his sexual desire and the probable outcome of this passion: death. It is a suicidal urge (as Hernández has told us so frequently before). The short versicle—which is at the exact center of the poem, with six stanzas and forty verses preceding it, and six stanzas and thirty-nine verses following it—is the turning point of the poem. It describes the object and only satisfaction of his desire: the woman whom he addresses. Caught between the axe (the destructive aspect of the feminine) and the rock (her enduring, eternal aspect) he has no choice. He must copulate with her. In the second half of the poem he alternately threatens this reluctant partner ("I Call Myself Mud" is similar in this respect) and tries to soften her both with descriptions of his certain annihilation if she does not yield, and with frequent mention of his need to perpetuate his forebears. Both in this poem and in "Bloody Fate" blood symbolizes passion, the passion which it was Hernández's fate to inherit, the passion which will sustain him, impel him, and finally kill him.

Another important motif in "My Blood Is a Road" is one which we first mentioned in our analysis of "The Well—*Alive*": that of the enclosure, confinement, or encasing of a vital force. Its first mention in this poem is in the perplexing second stanza, where blood is called a blouse (encasing), a cape (encasing) *within* his bones (doubly encased, within his body and within his bones), a constrictor (encasing) which bears anguish through (encased) his veins. This imagery is further complicated by the next stanza, with a fountain of necklaces or cords and cowbells (encasing) desiring to occupy (be encased in) her neck. The necklace or cord would surely encircle her neck, but the word "occupy" changes this entirely: the necklaces would like to be inside her neck. These seemingly paradoxical images of containers contained can all be explained logically when we realize that he is talking in both stanzas about his engorged phallus, its exterior like a blouse over the swollen capillaries within. Desire is within his bones and it squeezes him from without as well, bringing him to real physical pain. In the second stanza it is an upraised fountain, filled with circlets ("a magical deposit of rings," he later calls his sperm) which would like to fill her "neck" or canal. Just as with most of Hernández's major symbols, the motif of containment will be used in later periods to describe wholly different realities—jails and hatred, for example. The important thing is the fact that he continued to view reality through such a concept, with all its connotations of subjugation or suppression.

Such, then, was the first and longest period in Miguel Hernández's production. Many critics have dismissed this whole phase as a necessary but quickly surpassed apprenticeship, or even as self-deception: "Never has a poet been so false to himself as in *Expert in*

Moons," Arturo del Hoyo wrote in his prologue to the *Obra escogida (Selected Works)* of Miguel Hernández (Madrid: Aguilar, 1952, p. 12). José Ángel Valente goes further, indicting not only the mannered *Expert in Moons* but the critically acclaimed *Unending Thunderbolt* as well. Only with the war poetry, Valente writes, do we "discover an Hernández freed of the tyranny of his own verbal gifts, capable of infusing his poetry with the sense of a new and profound enthrallment rather than shooting it off futilely at the tangled labyrinth of the Baroque pastiche." He continues, characterizing *Thunderbolt* as "the culmination of the Orihuelan shepherd's enthusiasm for the traditional," "a perfect book [shunted off] on a siding, substantially imitative of the most tortuous mannerisms of the Baroque love lyric."[44] Vicente Gaos writes in a similar vein (both he and Valente are poets in their own right; their criticism smacks of disciples disappointed—or pleased?— to find that their master has faults): by virtue of his coming of literary age during the Gongorine revival, Miguel's natural gifts were irremediably perverted. "Thus, unavoidably, his poetry strikes me as an error, with a great disparity between what it could, *should* have been . . . and the expression it took. . . . There is in this *oeuvre* a disappointment, a misinterpretation, a turning away from the goal at which it seemed to aim."[45]

Certainly the later work of Hernández would be very different from this, and in many ways better—more original, with a vision less mediated through others' eyes. Yet is it unfair (and critically unsound) to criticize this period because it is unlike that later work. The boy struggles with a reality that is not the man's. If this poetry was mimetic in form and technique, it was also original in language and subject matter. From the first adolescent strivings to the last of the transitional poems, it tells the archetypal story of the young man struggling to find and define himself, to break the hold of that which would bind or limit him to the old ways, to old dependencies. Paradoxically, he tells this story in the old genres, decants the new wine in old vessels.

CHAPTER 3

The War Years (1936–39)

I *Biographical Data*

THE six months between the publication of *The Unending Thunderbolt* and the outbreak of the Spanish Civil War were important ones for Hernández. He and Josefina were reconciled after almost a year of estrangement. He continued to work on the taurine encyclopedia, although Madrid had begun to pall and he was looking for any kind of job which would enable him to be closer to Josefina. He worked on *The Comeliest Peasant*, about which he was enthusiastic because, as he wrote: "I know that it will be produced quickly, but above all because I'm creating the main character, the two central characters in the work, in my image and likeness, as I feel I am and would like to be" (cited in Ifach, pp. 174–75). He and Josefina exchanged long letters planning his visit to Orihuela in late July.

War broke out on July 18, but for several weeks life continued rather normally. Miguel went to Orihuela as planned. He found himself disagreeing politically with many of his friends, and he criticized "the pacific and abulic atmosphere" (Ifach, p. 177) of the village. On August 13, Josefina's father, a Civil Guard, was killed by Republican sympathizers: the young couple could no longer postpone the war's disruption of their lives. Miguel enlisted in the Republican army, and spent several months digging trenches, preparing the fortifications around Madrid. The close contact with his fellow soldiers undoubtedly helped Hernández when he sought to write verse and drama for the people. For although he himself was of the lower classes, his verse had always been, as Zardoya says repeatedly, an attempt to rise above those circumstances. It had always been directed to a minority.

Within a few months Miguel's talents were put to better use by
the Republican army. He was transferred to a propaganda unit and
given the title of Commissar of Culture. He began to publish poetry
in various partisan magazines and in the news bulletins which were
printed at each of the fronts. He traveled incessantly, giving readings at the fronts and on the radio, organizing a variety of entertain-
ments for the soldiers, fighting when he was needed. In 1937 he
wrote and published *Teatro en la guerra (Wartime Theater)*, consist-
ing of four one-act plays. He was also writing *Viento del pueblo
(Wind of the People)*, his first collection of war poems. In March of
1937 he and Josefina were married. For months they had argued
about whether they would have the religious ceremony Josefina
wanted, or the civil one Miguel wanted. If the circumstances had
been more normal, Josefina would certainly have had her way, but it
was difficult for Miguel to get leave and the wedding was postponed
various times. Finally they were married, hastily, in a civil ceremony. Their honeymoon consisted of one night in Alicante, which
Hernández later evoked in the poem "Orillas de tu vientre"
("Shores of Your Womb," *Complete Poetic Works*, pp. 399–400):

> Aún me estremece el choque primero de los dos;
> cuando hicimos pedazos la luna a dentelladas,
> impulsamos las sábanas a un abril de amapolas,
> nos inspiraba el mar.

> That first collision of the two still stirs me;
> When we tore the moon to shreds with our teeth,
> We impelled the sheets into an April of poppies,
> The sea inspired us.

They had lived together in Jaén for six weeks when Josefina's
recently widowed mother died. Only twenty-one herself, Josefina
suddenly had full responsibility for her three younger sisters and a
brother. She returned to Cox. Miguel writes her, in words which
remind us of two poems of his *Cancionero y romancero de ausencias
(Songs and Ballads of Absence*, Nos. 59 and 69), that her aroma
lingers on in their bedroom and in the bedclothes. He cannot understand why their happiness should be so short-lived, except that "he
who is born unlucky will always be dogged by misfortune" (cited in
Ifach, p. 196).

She soon discovered that she was pregnant, and Miguel's joy knew no bounds. He composed the poem (which was to become so famous) "Canción del esposo soldado"[1] ("Song of the Soldier Spouse"):

> He poblado tu vientre de amor y sementera,
> he prolongado el eco de sangre a que respondo
> y espero sobre el surco como el arado espera:
> he llegado hasta el fondo.
> . . . .
> Escríbeme a la lucha, siénteme en la trinchera:
> aquí con el fusil tu nombre evoco y fijo,
> y defiendo tu vientre de pobre que me espera,
> y defiendo tu hijo.
>
> Nacerá nuestro hijo con el puño cerrado,
> envuelto en un clamor de victoria y guitarras,
> y dejaré a tu puerta mi vida de soldado
> sin colmillos ni garras. (pp. 301–02)

> I have peopled your womb with love and seed,
> I have prolonged the echo of blood to which I respond
> And I wait over the furrow as the plow waits.
> I have plumbed the depths.
> . . . .
> Write to me at the front, think of me in the trenches:
> Here with my gun I evoke and fix your name,
> And I defend your poor woman's womb which awaits me
> And I defend your son.
>
> Our son will be born with a closed fist [the Republican salute],
> Swaddled in the clamor of victory and guitars,
> And I will leave at your door my soldier's life,
> Without fangs or claws.

In this poem and in a letter written at the same time (cited in Ifach, p. 197) he tells Josefina that she now seems made of glass, for she is fragile and her contents are precious. This motif will reappear in the "Last Poems," where he sings of her as "claridad absoluta, transparencia redonda" ("absolute clarity, rounded transparency," p. 413), and as "Cuerpo de claridad que nada empaña. / Todo es materia de cristal radiante" ("Body of a clarity which nothing dims. /

All is material of radiant crystal," p. 426). Weakened by constantly
overworking himself, Hernández began to suffer from what the doctors called cerebral anemia. Its symptoms were intense headaches
and debilitation.

In June he helped to organize and participated in the International Congress of Writers, which drew prominent writers from all
over the world, including Stephen Spender, André Malraux,
Nicolás Guillén, Octavio Paz, and César Vallejo. In August he
traveled to Moscow with a government-sponsored group of intellectuals to attend the Fifth Festival of Soviet Theater. They toured
Russia for more than a month, attending cultural events, receptions,
and banquets, giving interviews, writing for local newspapers. Two
mediocre poems, both included in the book *El hombre acecha (Man
the Spy)*, are a direct result of the trip: "La fábrica-cuidad" ("The
Factory City"), and "Rusia." So too is "España en ausencia" ("Spain
from Afar").

> De la extensión de Rusia, de sus tiernas ventanas,
> sale una voz profunda de máquinas y manos,
> que indica entre mujeres: *Aquí están tus hermanas,*
> y prorrumpe entre hombres: *Éstos son tus hermanos.*
> . . . .
> Hoy que contra mi patria clavan sus bayonetas
> legiones malparidas por una torpe entraña,
> los girasoles rusos, como ciegos planetas,
> hacen girar su rostro de rayos hacia España. ("Rusia," p. 318–19).

> From the breadth of Russia, from her tender windows,
> There comes a deep voice of machines and hands,
> Which among women says: *Here are your sisters,*
> And bursts out among men: *These are your brothers.*
> . . . .
> Today when legions ill-sprung from sluggish innards
> Sink their bayonets in my fatherland,
> The Russian sunflowers, like blind planets,
> Turn their face full of rays toward Spain. ("Russia")

He returned from Russia and left almost immediately for Teruel,
where he was on the front lines during that long, cold siege. He
apparently had no time to write to Josefina, although her confinement was imminent. He did not learn of the birth of his son, Manuel

(for Josefina's father) Ramón (for Sijé) until he returned home,[2] whereupon his joy can hardly be described; it filled his later, retrospective poetry:

> Fué una alegría de una sola vez,
> de esas que no son nunca más iguales.
> El corazón, lleno de historias tristes,
> fué arrebatado por las claridades.
> . . . .
> Fué la primera vez de la alegría,
> la sola vez de su total imagen.
> Las otras alegrías se quedaron
> como granos de arena entre los mares. (pp. 384–85)
> . . . .
> It was a joy only experienced once,
> A joy which can never be equaled.
> The heart, filled with its sad histories,
> Was swept away by the brightness.
>
> It was the first time of joy,
> The only time it was ever whole.
> Other joys became
> Like grains of sand in the seas.

He was able during the winter to spend a few weeks with his family, because the doctors had prescribed rest to cure his recurrent headaches. The memory of that time with his young son and his nursing wife also echoes through his later poetry.

> En la casa había enarcado
> la felicidad sus bóvedas.
> Dentro de la casa había
> siempre una luz victoriosa. (p. 382)
>
> In the house happiness
> Had arched its vaults.
> Within the house there was
> Always a victorious light.

He was assigned to the Army of the Coast for a few months, then transferred again in June. He continued to write and to give recitations although he was "exhausted physically and morally from the

constant coming and going, and there was no immediate goal or end
which might have animated his spirit and his conscience," Ifach
writes from her memory of him (p. 221). He was writing the poems
which would constitute *Man the Spy*, poems in which this exhaustion is patent.

The Republican position was becoming more and more untena-
ble; the resultant fears and doubts among the men made it difficult
for the sensitive Hernández to continue with his propaganda activities. Moreover, his small son was ill and Josefina was pregnant
again: neither had enough to eat. In October the ten-month-old
child, weakened by months of an intestinal disorder and malnutri-
tion, worsened and died. Miguel was desolated. Josefina in her
mourning withdrew from everything around her. His anguish and
hers are re-created again and again in Miguel's poetry of the period.

> Fué una alegría para siempre sola,
> para siempre dorada, destellante.
> Pero es una tristeza para siempre,
> porque apenas nacida fué a enterrarse. (p. 385)

> It was a joy forever unique,
> Forever golden, forever dazzling.
> But it is a sadness forever,
> Because scarcely born it went to its grave.

> Yo No quisiera que toda
> aquella luz se alejara
> vencida desde la alcoba.

> Pero cuando llueve, siento
> que el resplandor se desploma,
> y reverdecen los muebles
> despintados por las gotas.

> Memorias de la alegría,
> cenizas latentes, doran
> alguna vez las paredes
> plenas de la triste historia.

> Pero la casa no es,
> no puede ser, otra cosa
> que un ataúd con ventanas,
> . . . .

En la casa falta un cuerpo
que aleteaban las alondras.
. . . .
En la casa falta un cuerpo
que en la tierra se desborda. (pp. 382–83)

I would not have wished that all
That light retreat
Vanquished from the bedroom.

But when it rains, I feel
That the splendor crumbles,
And the furniture faded
By the drops greens again.
Memories of happiness,
Latent ashes, at times
Gild the walls so
Full of the sad story.

But the house is not,
Cannot be, anything but
A coffin with windows,
. . . .
In the house a body is missing
Which the swallows made flutter.
. . . .
In the house a body is missing
Which overflows in the earth.

The war was drawing to its bloody and inevitable close, but Miguel refused to make any plans presupposing the defeat of the Republic. Such blind loyalty or stubborn integrity characterized— and doomed—him. He was as uncompromising in his political commitment as he had been in his passion for Josefina: his blood *was* a road. His friends recall him in those last months of the war "somnambulant and disconcerted at the general collapse which was presenting itself, and too generous and ingenuous" to believe what everyone around him was saying (Cano Ballesta, p. 51). He went on writing the poems which compose *Man the Spy* (which would not be published in his lifetime and which was not published in Spain until 1976, after Franco's death) wherein he vented his desolation and pessimism in his own way. In its dedication to Neruda he wrote:

"Pablo: A somber rose bush approaches and hovers over me, over a familiar crib whose bottom is falling out piece by piece until within it we can make out not just a child of suffering, but the depths of the earth. . . . You inquire about the heart, and I do, too. Look at all the mouths ashen from rancor, hunger, death, pale from not singing, not laughing: dried up from not surrendering to the profound kiss. But look at the *pueblo* [this word means both people and nation in Spanish] which smiles with its florid sadness, auguring the future of joyous being . . ." (p. 313).

In January Josefina bore him another son, Manuel Miguel (nicknamed Manolo):

> Rueda que irás muy lejos.
> Ala que irás muy alto.
> Torre del día, niño.
> Alborear del pájaro.
>
> Niño: ala, rueda, torre.
> Pie. Pluma. Espuma. Rayo.
> Ser como nunca ser.
> . . . .
> Asciende. Rueda. Vuela,
> creador de alba y mayo.
> Galopa. Ven. Y colma
> el fondo de mis brazos. (pp. 380–81)
>
> Wheel that will range so far.
> Wing that will soar so high.
> Tower of daylight, child.
> Dawning of the bird.
>
> Child: wing, wheel, tower.
> Foot. Feather. Froth. Lightning.
> Being as it has never been.
> . . . .
> Soar. Roll. Fly,
> Creator of dawn and May.
> Gallop. Come. And fill to overflowing
> The depths of my arms.

The war ended on March 29, 1939. Hernández finally sought refuge in the Embassy of Chile, where Neruda had been consul when they first became friends. He despised the thought of leaving

Spain and had made no plans for Josefina and Manolo. When the attaché hesitated about whether or not he could be given asylum, Hernández fled the embassy. He returned to Cox, passing first through Valencia to get a copy of *Man the Spy*—printed but unbound—to give to Josefina for safekeeping. He spent almost three weeks with his family before setting out for Portugal and refuge. He did manage to cross the border but was quickly detained by the Portuguese police, who returned him to the Spanish Civil Guard without delay or consideration for his status as a political refugee. His life as a prisoner had begun.

II *The Writings of the War Years*

The prose work of this period is composed of the dedications to the two books of poetry and to *Wartime Theater*. Hernández also wrote numerous articles about "aspects of the life in the vanguard and in the rear guard, at the front and in the city" (Ifach, p. 195) for various newspapers. These articles—sometimes pseudonymous—have recently been published by Juan Cano Ballesta and Robert Marrast in *Poesía y prosa de guerra y otros textos olvidados*. Primarily reportorial, they will not be analyzed here.

The poetry consists of twenty-five poems in *Wind of the People*, eighteen poems in *Man the Spy*, and six other poems which appear in the *Complete Works* as "Other Poems, 1938–39." In addition, the poems "Smile at Me" and "Dawn of the Hatchets" which were written on the eve of the war, might well be considered part of the second period rather than transitional. J. Lechner describes "Smile at Me" as "not only the poem in which Miguel Hernández distances himself from the Church but also and above all a definitive declaration of solidarity with the people, the result of a spiritual maturation in the poet and of the influences of Alberti and Neruda: it is a clearly marked [turning] point in his poetic work."[3]

Drama is the largest component of this period: there are two peasant plays,[4] *Sons of Stone* and *The Comeliest Peasant;* the four one-act plays of *Wartime Theater;* and *El pastor de la muerte (The Shepherd of Death)*, which is a combination peasant and propaganda play.

The works of the war years are set apart dramatically from Hernández's earlier and later writing. His conception of the poet's function and relation to society had changed radically from his days in

Orihuela. Since this change greatly affected his art, we will consider it in some detail. In the style and diction of his transitional poems we first perceive Hernández's rejection of "pure" poetry in the Symbolist tradition, with its excessive aestheticism (exaltation and creation of beauty for its own sake) and its deification of the poet, in favor of Neruda's avowedly "impure" poetry, poetry which dealt with the everyday realities. From the espousal of impure poetry, it was only a step for Hernández to embrace the Marxist idea that the artist has a social responsibility and moral duty to speak of, for, and to the people. Hernández was, after all, of the people himself. (It is ironic that it took the efforts of the upper-middle-class intellectuals with whom he associated in Madrid to convince him of this duty to his own class.[5]) In "Smile at Me" he declares:

> Sonreídme, que voy
> adonde estáis vosotros los de siempre,
> los que cubrís de espigas y racimos la boca del que nos escupe,
> los que conmigo en surcos, andamios, fraguas, hornos,
> os arrancáis la corona del sudor a diario.
> . . . .
> salté al monte de donde procedo,
> a las viñas donde halla tanta hermana mi sangre,
> a vuestra compañía de relativo barro. (pp. 258–59)

> Smile at me, because I am coming
> To where you have always been,
> You who cover with spikes of grain and grape clusters the mouth
>   of the one who spits on us,
> You who with me in the furrows, scaffolds, smithies, blast furnaces,
> Wrest from yourselves a crown of sweat each day.
> . . . .
> I leapt up to the mountain whence I came,
> To the vineyards where my blood finds its brothers,
> To your company of related mud.

He speaks—with a vocabulary by now familiar to us—of putting all his previous passion at the disposal of this new cause:

> Agrupo mi hambre, mis penas y estas cicatrices
> que llevo de tratar piedras y hachas,
> a vuestras hambres, vuestras penas y vuestra herrada carne,
> porque para calmar nuestra desesperación de toros castigados
> habremos de agruparnos oceánicamente. (p. 259)

> I join my hunger, my sorrows, and these scars
> I wear from my dealings with stones and axes,
> To your hungers, your sorrows, and your branded flesh,
> Because to calm our desperation of castigated bulls
> We will have to join together oceanically.

In the dedication of *Wind of the People* to Aleixandre, Hernández describes the poet as a man chosen to be spokesman for the *pueblo*. "Vicente: Life has made us, who among all men were born poets, poets at the side of all men. . . . Our source will always be the same: the earth. Our destiny is to end up in the hands of the *pueblo* [people]. Only those honest hands can hold what the honest blood of the poet pours vibrantly forth . . ." (p. 263).

Lechner writes that the committed Republican artists "rejected decisively any form of directorship in art, and it has been shown that even in the case of those who seemed active in the Communist Party (we are talking about the major poets: those we have treated in these pages), they did not 'produce' according to party directives nor did they even create an art in line with Communist doctrine" (I, 253–54). Yet if we cannot classify Hernández's objectives as doctrinaire Marxism, they were close to being so. He was one poet who did not shy away from directing the people: "We poets are the wind of the *pueblo*. We are born to go blowing through their pores and to direct their eyes and their feelings toward the most beautiful heights. Today, this day of passion, of life, of death, irresistibly impels you, me, many of us, toward the *pueblo*. The people await the poets with ears and souls attentive . . .," he continued in his dedication.

As the war progressed, Hernández became more committed, closer to dogmatic Marxism. Lechner writes: "The times in which this poetry was written were not propitious for poets' reflections about the aesthetic problems of their own art: thus it is that in the Balladbook [of Republican war ballads] as well as here [in *Hora de España*, the best of the poetry reviews] there is no *ars poetica* [poetic manifesto]. What did occupy the mind of almost all the Republican artists involved in the conflict, was the relationship between the artist and his audience, the problem of communication between the two, and the problem of the committed artist, questions which were generally formulated explicitly and in prose" (I, 196). Hernández did consider these problems in prose, as we have seen, but he wrote an *ars poetica* in verse as well, "Llamo a los poetas" ("I Call Out to the Poets"), in which he addresses most of his fellow Republican poets, asking them to join him in his commitment:[6]

> Dejemos el museo, la biblioteca, el aula
> sin emoción, sin tierra, glacial, para otro tiempo.
> Ya sé que en esos sitios tiritará mañana
> mi corazón helado en varios tomos.
> ....
> Abandonemos la solemnidad.
> Así: sin esa barba postiza, ni esa cita
> que la insolencia pone bajo nuestra nariz,
> hablaremos unidos, comprendidos, sentados,
> de las cosas del mundo frente al hombre.
>
> Así descenderemos de nuestro pedestal,
> de nuestra pobre estatua. Y a cantar entraremos
> a una bodega, a un pecho, o al fondo de la tierra,
> sin el brillo del lente polvoriento. (p. 337)

> Let us leave the museum, the library, the classroom
> So unfeeling, otherworldly, glacial, for another time.
> I know that tomorrow in those places my heart,
> Frozen, will shiver in various volumes.
> ....
> Let us abandon solemnity.
>
> Thus: without that fake beard, or that quotation
> Which insolence puts under our nose,
> We will talk united, comprehended, seated,
> Of the things of the world in relation to man.
>
> Thus will we descend from our pedestal,
> From our poor statue. And to sing we will enter
> Some tavern, breast, or the depths of the earth,
> Without the glint of a dusty magnifying glass.

In the introduction to *Wartime Theater* Hernández enunciates even more emphatically his allegiance to the ideal of proletarian art:

I believe that drama is a magnificent weapon of war against the traitors who face us and those at home. I understand that all drama, all poetry, all art, must be, today more than ever, a weapon of war. . . . With my poetry and my drama, the two weapons most suited to me and most used by me, I try to clear the head and the heart of my *pueblo*. . . . In my poetry, in my theater, I show the struggles of my passions, which reflect those of the rest of you, and I always strive to have the pure understanding of them triumph. Within the breast of each one of us, those of us who fight for the revolution, striving, perfecting itself is the revolution, which begins to burst forth helped more by interior strength than exterior.

I say to myself: if the world is a theater, if the revolution is flesh of the theater, let us endeavor to make the theater, and thereby the revolution, exemplary, and perhaps, no, *surely* we will among all of us succeed in making the world that way as well.

I say to myself; we must bury the ruins of the obscene and lying theater of the bourgeoisie, of all the bourgeoisies and comforts of the soul, which are still around kicking up dust and ruination in our midst. . . . (pp. 807–08)

It is natural, then, in the light of Hernández's committed ideals, that his work in this period would differ markedly from that of his first period. To begin with structural elements, we find that the genres he used are different. The three examples of prose are not poetically descriptive vignettes, but transcriptions of poetic conversations with Aleixandre and Neruda, or, in the case of the introduction to *Wartime Theater*, an hortatory speech. These three pieces are so minor that they could not be said to constitute a genre in this period; their principal interest is not literary but biographical.

The poetry of the war years is principally *arte mayor*, that is, thirty-six poems (including "Smile at Me") out of fifty have verses longer than octosyllables. These poems do not use the *culto* forms which dominated the first period; there are only two sonnets, both alexandrine (fourteen syllables) rather than hendecasyllabic. In fact, the alexandrine line becomes frequent, used at first (in *Wind of the People*) in free combination with hendecasyllables and heptasyllables—the same combinations Hernández used in the transitional poems—and later by itself, or combined with a *pie quebrado* (hemistich). The hendecasyllables were also combined with himistiches in the later work, *Man the Spy*, where free groupings of verses—Neruda's versicles—have disappeared from the *arte mayor* in favor of the thoroughly traditional quatrain.

The *arte menor* consists of fourteen poems, nine of them octosyllabic, five heptasyllabic. According to Lechner this subordination of *arte menor* to *arte mayor* was generalized among the Republican poets.[7] He conjectures that they may have heeded Rosa Chacal's evaluation of the *romance* (octosyllabic ballad) as a vehicle for war poetry: *romances* and bombers cannot coexist (I, 200). Nonetheless the *romances* that were written became very popular: they were anthologized, set to music, played on the radio and in movies, and learned by the blind streetcorner musicians.[8] All but two of Hernández's appear in his earlier collection, *Wind of the People,* when he was undoubtedly still experimenting to find the best verse for communicating his message. The drawback of the ballad as a serious persuasive tool is evident: its short verse and obligatory assonance give it a quick rhythmic pace unsuited to explication. In his study of the Spanish Civil War ballad, Puccini discerns two fundamental tonalities in the ballads produced: (1) "descriptive realism, crude or tender, of the war—which is always hard and bitter"; and (2) the "unpitying or ironic invective—Quevedesque—against traitors and treason." The works of Rafael Alberti and José Bergamín fall into the latter category, he believes, whereas "the lyrical, pathetic and dolorous accents of Hernández or of Prados" fall into the first (*Le romancero. . .* , p. 53). Only one of Hernández's ballads, "Los cobardes" ("The Cowards"), is clearly Quevedesque in its vulgar and imprecatory tone.

The alexandrine line and the quatrain (slightly varied by the hemistich) came to be Hernández's most typical poetic "weapons." They offered him the best possibility for delivering a clear, almost conversational, message.

The drama which Hernández wrote in this period of political commitment was meant for the stage, whereas the *auto sacramental,* like much of the early poetry, had been more an exercise in aesthetics and formalism. Hernández judged the theater, as Sijé had, an ideal medium for persuasion, as we have seen in his introduction to *Wartime Theater.* In that introduction he described his peasant plays as "plays exalting work and condemning the bourgeoisie" (p. 807). *Wartime Theater* was a "weapon of war," as was *Shepherd of Death.* With *Wartime Theater* Hernández believed he had initiated a new dramatic genre: "One of my ways of fighting is to have begun cultivating a short and cutting drama: a wartime drama. *La cola* [*The Line*], *El hombrecito* [*The Little Man*], *El refugiado* [*The Refugee*], *Los sentados* [*The Sitters*], are examples of the theater which I have begun" (p. 807). Actually, although the length of these playlets—ranging from 114 to 150 lines of dialogue—was uncommonly short, their allegorical style and didactic aim certainly assimilated them to Hernández's *auto sacramental.*

In his choice of genres and poetic forms during the war years, Hernández manifested his belief that the poet must be the "wind of the people," leading them on toward the revolution. His prose was unadorned, his poetry conversational or traditional, his drama conventional, or in the case of *Wartime Theater*, simplistically allegorical. In all cases, communication was the principal objective. If we were to use Northrop Frye's theory of genres, we would have to say that Hernández used only one genre in this period (with the exception of *Sons of Stone* and *The Comeliest Peasant*), for the prose, most of the poetry, and the last two dramas fall under Frye's definition of *epos:* "In *epos*, the author confronts his audience directly, and the hypothetical characters of his story are concealed" (*Anatomy of Criticism*, p. 249). Because of the presence of the "Voice of the Poet" in *Wartime Theater* and *Shepherd of Death*, they do not fulfill Frye's definition of drama: "in drama, the hypothetical or internal characters of the story confront the audience directly, hence the drama is marked by the concealment of the author from his audience" (p. 249). Only in the prewar *Sons of Stone* and *The Comeliest Peasant* does Hernández "conceal" himself from the audience.

III Vocabulary and Syntax

There is a marked change in the vocabulary of this period, in keeping with the change of audience and objective. The vocabulary is simple and free of neologisms. The new elements are vulgarisms—scatological, blasphemous, or sexual—and, naturally enough, words related to the war. There is an entire poem based on the relatively vulgar topic of sweat ("El sudor"), which Hernández—ever the metaphorist—calls "rain of the axillas," "manna of men," with its "fecund odors," and its "sword of savory crystals." (Hernández once mentioned this poem and "Las manos" ["The Hands"] as two among his war poems which had come closest to expressing what he wanted to say [Ifach, p. 221].)

Hernández had used vulgar language in earlier poetry, notably "The Whistling Song of Affirmation in the Village" (pp. 182–87), and had written about vulgar subject matter (outhouses, sexual arousal, masturbation), but never as consistently as during the war years. He was notoriously foul-mouthed in person, so it is not surprising that in a period when colloquial speech was considered apt, even desirable, for poetry, Hernández should let slip numerous vulgarisms. From the aesthetic point of view, Hernández's use of clichés in the war poetry is equally lamentable. Puccini considers it one of the few faults to be found in this poetry:

Of course if on the one hand the experience [of writing] militant poetry—which must be read and listened to—frees Hernández definitively from some literary obstacles and limbers and lightens his poetic diction, on the other hand it frequently weakens this diction with the adoption of various popular beliefs or myths (the myth of virility, unarmed heroism, of the dead who are more alive than the living, etc.), or with the not always felicitous use of the so-called lexicalized metaphors ("dolor a rienda suelta" ["sorrow with a free rein"], "no hay madera para tanto ataúd" ["there's not enough wood for so much coffin"], "nunca se pondrá el sol sobre su frente" ["the sun will never set over his brow"], etc.), and because of the use of some sententious forms, which are nonetheless sometimes quite pretty ("varios tragos es la vida, y un solo trago la muerte" ["life is a few drafts, and death but one"]; "morir es lo más grande que se hace" ["dying is the greatest thing we do"]; "es preciso matar para seguir viviendo" ["one must kill in order to go on living"]; "si no se pierde todo, no se ha perdido nada" ["if everything is not lost, nothing is lost"], etc.). (pp. 83–84)

Hernández was far from alone in this reliance on commonplaces, as Lechner's study clearly shows. The majority of the Republican poets were aware of the artistic dangers implicit in writing engaged poetry: "the poets realize . . . that in the atmosphere of war and agitation words are frequently weakened by their propagandistic burden and in any case are not able to encompass all the drama of the war, much less to explain it so that it will make sense to those who have suffered it unwillingly; they know that their own words frequently serve an ideology, a faction . . . and that they barely have the opportunity or the possibility of forging their poetry in an atmosphere uncontaminated by the pressure of the urgency of immediate ends . . ." (I, 196–97).

The nadir of Hernández's use of vulgarities and clichés is *Wartime Theater*, whose component plays seem little more than sentences of propaganda—improprieties and bromides strung loosely together. In the case of these plays we can affirm without hesitation that literary norms have been abandoned: they are propaganda, not literature. With the remainder of the war production such an affirmation is not possible, and so we must judge it by literary standards, something which many of Hernández's critics and biographers have been unwilling to do. Zardoya, Williams, Ifach, and Couland[9] speak of his passionate involvement in the cause and of his "sincerity," as though these constituted artistic merits in themselves. They do not; they should be (insofar as possible) irrelevant to our judgment of his work. Puccini criticizes some aspects of this war work, as we have seen, but his neohumanist literary philosophy leads him to consider best those works which reflect the author's humanity most nakedly. In general, then, he judges the war poetry favorably. Guerrero Zamora is the only critic who has openly condemned the work of this period, and he has done so for equally subjective reasons: he did not agree with Miguel's politics.

In general, the syntax of the poems is discoursive. Especially in the alexandrines and the poems with seven-eleven-fourteen-syllable combinations, the length of the verses allows a close approximation to speech. There is little hyperbaton, and ellipsis is minimal. Lechner speaks of a similar evolution in the poetry of Alberti and Prados, motivated by their desire to speak to the common man: "This desire can be seen in the frequent use of popular poetic forms, a simple vocabulary and frequent apostrophes, questions, and incitations to the reader; the syntax—axis of the problem of 'obscurity' in poetry—is usually uncomplicated" (I, 125).

The plays vary considerably. *Sons of Stone* is a prose drama with a great deal of figurative language and a syntax more poetic than prosaic. There is some hyperbaton, although it is not as radical as it was in the early period. *The Comeliest Peasant* is by far the most successful and the most poetic of Hernández's plays. While it does not lack a political message, art—not propaganda—is its *raison d'être*. The syntax is not difficult, but we find some hyperbaton and ellipsis. Certainly these were mandated in part by the short, popular poetic forms which Hernández used in this play (for an inventory of these forms, see Zardoya, p. 709), as well as by his desire to imitate the poetic diction of Lope and Lorca.

> Yo sé
> que donde pone su pie,
> derretirse como cera
> a las piedras se las ve. (p. 674)
> . . .
> Ten para el principio y ten
> paciencia para el final. (p. 722)

I know
That where he puts his foot
To melt like wax
The rocks are seen.
. . .
Have for the beginning and have
Patience for the end.

The syntax of much of *Wartime Theater* is colloquial or substandard. There is little action or description in the plays; each consists of one scene on the home front during the war. There is a variety of characters, always divided into two groups—the cowards and the partisans. These figures discuss their feelings about the war, and the partisans triumph verbally. Hernández tried to reproduce the flavor of common speech, repetitious, hackneyed and ungrammatical.

In *Shepherd of Death*, which represents something of a synthesis of the peasant and proletarian plays, Hernández once again used traditional verse forms. To a certain extent this *arte menor* (use of short lines) precludes a conversational syntax, so that hyperbaton and ellipsis appear with relative frequency. We can only surmise the reason for this change, a change also evident in some of the poems written, as *Shepherd of Death* was, near the end of the war. In "Canción primera" ("First Song"), "Canción última" ("Last Song"), "Carta" ("Letter"), "El tren de los heridos" ("The Train of the Wounded"), and "18 de julio 1936–18 de julio 1938" ("July 18, 1936–July 18, 1938"), there is a similar return to a more elliptical, connotative style, with felicitous results. Perhaps Hernández finally realized that his audience had always loved and understood traditional poetry—in spite or because of its enigmatic nature; perhaps he was disillusioned with proletarian art altogether. His proselytizing stage was over. In "Last Song" as he turns his eyes symbolically away from the war, we see the elliptical style emerging:

Pintada, no vacía:
pintada está mi casa
del color de las grandes
pasiones y desgracias.

Regresará del llanto
adonde fué llevada
con su desierta mesa,
con su ruinosa cama.

Florecerán los besos
sobre las almohadas.
Y en torno de los cuerpos
elevará la sábana
su intensa enredadera
nocturna, perfumada.

El odio se amortigua
detrás de la ventana.

Será la garra suave.

Dejadme la esperanza. (p. 343)

Painted, not empty:
Painted, my house
With the color of the great
Passions and sorrows.

It will return from the weeping
Where it was borne
With its deserted table,
With its ruinous bed.

Kisses will flower
On the pillows.
And all about the bodies
The sheet will raise
Its intense vine
Nocturnal and perfumed.

Hate dies down
Beyond the window

The claw will be soft.

Leave me the hope.

IV *Figurative Language*

The figurative language of the war years differs significantly from
that of the first period because it lacks any pretense to wittiness (that
clever poetic self-consciousness so prized in the seventeenth century, which Hernández had imitated in his Neo-Gongorine phase).

If he had sought once to create poetry which was "a beautiful affected lie" whose aim was "illustrating sensations" or "dazzling the
mind with the flashes of a perfectly tailored image" (see above,
p. 30, he now pursued what he had, in that early manifesto, identified
as its opposite: "prophetic" poetry. As he foresaw then, "clarity is
essential" to prophetic verse, for its aim is "spreading emotions and
inflaming lives."

As early as the peasant plays, transitional in many respects, the
metaphors have been pruned of artifice.

> Pocas flores, mayo,
> diste a mi vergel:
> ¡la del amor mío
> no va a florecer! (p. 672)

> Few flowers, May,
> Did you give my garden:
> That of my love
> Is not going to bloom!

"¡Ay, qué frío, qué frío! son una sementera de hielo mis huesos y mi corazón . . . Estoy a punto de quedarme cuajada como un charco . . ." (p. 645).

"Oh, the cold, the cold! My bones and my heart are a field sown with
ice . . . In a moment I shall freeze over like a puddle. . . ."

In the war poetry and drama, the metaphors have been reduced to
little more than emblems of good or evil, Republican or Nationalist,
male or unmale. Synecdoche (a figure in which the part stands for
the whole: the "pen" signifies literature which is mightier than the
"sword," signifying war; or vice versa: here comes the "law," i.e., a
policeman) is frequent. Allusion to any but the most widely known
figures has disappeared. Apostrophe or direct address is present in
forty-one of the fifty poems, an astonishing percentage, indicative of
Hernández's passion to communicate directly with his audience. It
should be borne in mind that most of this poetry was written for oral
delivery: apostrophe is a standard oratorical attention-getting device. We may divide the type of address into exhortation, directed
at the Republicans, or at potential allies, or at the as yet uncommit-
ted; and name-calling, directed at the Nationalists and their German
and Italian allies. Several of the most moving poems in the period

are the exhortatory "Vientos del pueblo me llevan" ("Winds of the People Carry Me") and "Aceituneros" ("Olive Workers"). In the first Hernández utilizes a device common to traditional poetry—the enumeration of place-names—to lend the force of tradition to his revolutionary message:

> Asturianos de braveza,
> vascos de piedra blindada,
> valencianos de alegría
> y castellanos de alma,
> labrados como la tierra
> y airosos como las alas;
> andaluces de relámpago,
> . . . .
> extremeños de centeno,
> gallegos de lluvia y calma,
> catalanes de firmeza,
> aragoneses de casta,
> murcianos de dinamita
> frutalmente propagada,
> leoneses, navarros, dueños
> del hambre, el sudor y el hacha,
> reyes de la minería,
> señores de la labranza,
> hombres que entre las raíces,
> como raíces gallardas,
> vais de la vida a la muerte,
> vais de la nada a la nada:
> yugos os quieren poner
> gentes de la hierba mala,
> yugos que habéis de dejar
> rotos sobre sus espaldas. (p. 271)

> Asturians of fierceness,
> Basques of armored rock,
> Valencians of joy
> And Castilians of soul,
> Worked like the earth
> And airy as wings;
> Andalusians of lightning bolts,
> . . . .
> Estremenians of rye,
> Galicians of rain and tranquility,

Catalonians of endurance,
Aragonese of caste,
Murcians of dynamite
Propagated like fruit trees,
Leonese, Navarrese, lords
Of hunger, sweat and the axe,
Kings of mining,
Masters of farming,
Men who amongst the roots,
Like noble roots,
Move from life to death
Move from nothing to nothing:
Yokes they would impose on you,
Those dissolute people,
Yokes that you must leave
Broken over their shoulders.

Hyperbole figures prominently in this poetry, as we might expect: the pejorative directed at the enemy, the laudatory at his comrades. Anaphora is used extensively, not often artistically, to hammer home the message. Anaphora, like apostrophe, is especially suited to poetry which is to be recited:

Que vienen, vienen, vienen
los lentos, lentos, lentos,
los ávidos, los fúnebres,
los aéreos carniceros.
. . . .
Que nadie, nadie, nadie
lo olvide ni un momento.
Que no es posible el crimen.
Que no es posible esto. (pp. 355–56)

They're coming, coming, coming,
The slow, slow, slow,
The avid, the funereal,
The airborne butchers.
. . . .
Let nobody, nobody, nobody
Forget it for one moment.
That crime is not possible.
That this is not possible.

Guerrero Zamora studies at some length the variety of reiterations, correlations and parallelisms that Hernández employs in the war poetry (pp. 281–88). He concludes that Hernández sought with these repetitions to heighten the emotional intensity of the work and at the same time to achieve a "special cadence, a rhythmical ritornello," although "at times such repetitions are nothing more than words repeated to fill out the verse, that is to say, padding" (p. 285).

There are two further figurative uses of language which stand out in this period: the use of visions and the corporealization of abstract entities. Both of these figures are familiar to us from the first period, but now we find the visions far more abundant. Daniel Williams describes one particular variety of vision (without identifying it as such). It is "the use of dynamic verbs of violent motion quite unrelated to their corresponding subjects in any normal frame of reference. This poetic recourse emphasizes . . . the chaotic substance of life and things during a time of war and bloodshed" (p. 171). He cites examples from "1° de mayo, 1937" ("Mayday, 1937"): plows bellow, carnations shoot, flowers boil. Zardoya says *Wind of the People* is characterized by an "enormous visionary force. There are visions which flash like lightning, Dantesque visions" (p. 676).

Cano Ballesta analyzes brilliantly both the visionary and corporealizing images in the war poetry (pp. 148–57). "The diction of Miguel Hernández, always terrestrial and corporeal, becomes weightier and harder, bathes itself in stone and metal. It is a return to a primitive, elemental world, to a world where realities impose themselves on the senses, through their weight and hardness" (p. 148). "Corporeal images, hard, metallic, of tools and weapons, are the expression of this implacable world at war: . . . 'eyes of granite,' . . . 'tears of steel,' . . . 'Like the forge which loses its hammer, / Manuel Moral is silent,' . . . 'Joy advances razing mountains / and mouths advance like shields,' . . . 'with my blood and my mouth / like two faithful guns' " (pp. 149–50). These visions, combined with frequent synaesthesia and continuous violations of semantic systems (i.e., joining together orders of words which are incongruous: "under a claw of rain / and a grape cluster of dew," p. 280) give these images "originality and overwhelming force" (p. 152).

Cano notes that while this corporealization continues into many of the poems of *Man the Spy,* another sort of metaphor comes to the fore in that work, one which describes man's dehumanization, his descent into bestiality: "He regresado al tigre" ("I have regressed to a tiger"), Hernández writes in "First Song," setting the tone of the collection. Simultaneously, nature is humanized, as are various machines (the train in "The Train of the Wounded," the airplane in "El vuelo de los hombres," ["The Flight of Men"], cities, objects, jails, factories, and blood.) In short, the human and nonhuman have changed places in a world turned upside down by war:

> Se ha retirado el campo
> Al ver abalanzarse
> crispadamente al hombre.
>
> ¡Qué abismo entre el olivo
> y el hombre se descubre!
> . . . .
> Hoy el amor es muerte,
> y el hombre acecha al hombre. (p. 315)
>
> The countryside has drawn back
> Seeing man paroxysmally
> Precipitate himself.
>
> What an abyss opens up
> Between the olive tree and man!
> . . . .
> Today love is death,
> And man is spying on man.

V Themes

The themes of the war period are far more easily (and less arbitrarily) identified than those of the first period, for in both form and themes Hernández sought utter clarity, denotation rather than connotation.

1. The war as purification. The struggle is characterized as one between good and evil, between solar and chthonic principles, between spirit and Mammon. The Manichean morality Hernández struggled against as a boy seems to have permanently informed his way of perceiving the world. José Valverde studies this aspect of the war poetry in his previously cited study (see Ch. II, n. 41).

2. Group solidarity. This is the predominant theme—and objective—of Hernández's writing. His own " 'conversion' to the collective world," as Puccini describes it (p. 62) was rapid and total (Hernández had many of the characteristics of Hoffer's "true believer"). This new solidarity which, Puccini continues, presupposed a change of "attitudes, of concepts, of perspectives" and went hand in hand with "changes in modes and forms," provoked two phenomena: "on the one hand, the confession is raised to the level of dialogue; on the other, the personal drama is exemplified on an epic level" (p. 85). Essentially, Hernández saw himself as Everyman in this war: when he was singing his own pain he sang that of his comrades as well. The shepherd of death is an autobiographical figure, but representative of all Republican soldiers.

Vicente Ramos writes of Hernández's deep love of "the poor, the disinherited of the earth" (p. 292), of his advocacy for the dignity of man. Hernández's verse, "un amor hacia todo me atormenta" ("my love for everything torments me," p. 228), "is, in short, truly the spinal cord of the life and of the work of Miguel Hernández" (p. 293). (Ramos's eagerness to prove that Hernández was never politically motivated, i.e., never a Communist, leads him into hyperbolic descriptions of the poet's altruism.) Hernández urged solidarity on his comrades and their allies by praising past examples of camaraderie, as in "Fuerza del Manzanares" ("Force of the Manzanares," pp. 308–10), "Al soldado internacional caído en España" ("To the International Soldier Fallen in Spain," pp. 288–89), or "Euzkadi" (usually spelled "Euskadi," this being the Basque name for their homeland), or by citing the example of Republican heroes, such as Lister, La Pasionaria, Pablo de la Torriente, and García Lorca. Many of these poems urge further solidarity by reminding the listeners of the exploitation and hardships they have borne as a class and as an army: "Sentado sobre los muertos" ("Sitting on the Dead," pp. 268–70), "Winds of the People Carry Me," "El niño yuntero" ("The Plowboy," pp. 272–74), considered by many to be one of the best social poems written during the war; "Jornaleros" ("Day Laborers," pp. 287–88), "Olive Workers" (pp. 289–90), "El soldado y la nieve" ("The Soldier and the Snow," pp. 322–23), and "El hambre" ("Hunger," pp. 325–27).

3. Need to defeat the enemy. This is a self-evident theme in war poetry, but Hernández develops it in an interesting way: he consistently portrays the enemy as feminine (using all of the archetypal

symbols for the feminine that we mentioned in Chapter 2) and the Republicans as masculine. The need for the male to overcome the power of the female is simply a continuation of the struggle Hernández sustained in earlier years against the pull of the unconscious.[10] As we noted in Theme 1, the antagonists in this struggle are identified like those of the first period, as solar and chthonic. Related to this theme is the motif of the overprotective mother, "the enemy at home," who will not allow her son to go off to war.

4. Need to supplant the enemy's doctrines. This is an intellectualized form of the physical battle of Theme 3. Capitalism, Fascism, and organized religion are reviled, while the opposing systems—Communism or Socialism—are exalted. Russia, Lenin, and Mayday are the subjects of poems. This form of struggle, the supplanting of the old law for the new, is also part of the archetype which dominates this period of Hernández's development.

5. Longing for a new order. This theme appears only in a few of the late poems and may be labeled transitional. Similar to the formal change toward connotation and ambiguity in the later poems, this thematic and tonal change betokens a fundamental change in Hernández's thinking.

At this point in our analysis a consideration of the archetypal patterns underlying Hernández's work will increase our understanding of that work. The Hero Myth is now the dominant archetype (for a full-length study of this archetype and its manifestations in world literature the reader is referred to Joseph Campbell's classic *The Hero with a Thousand Faces*). The mythic path of the young man begins as he fortifies himself against the pull of the unconscious (or Feminine) by alliance with other men. In his earlier struggles he was alone; now he joins a society of males who reinforce him in his drive toward the higher solar masculinity, banishing the chthonic or phallic. Hernández found this solidarity in his comrades-at-arms, whom he always describes in terms of light, sun, and purity.

Once the young man has been fortified in this way, he sets out to destroy the World Parents (those repressive forces, internal and external, which would impair his development). The slaying of the Great Mother, the destruction of her negative hold on him, is mythologically represented as a perilous descent into the underworld, or as being swallowed. It is only by exposing himself to this peril that the man can vanquish the destructive Great Mother, thereby liberating "the Captive," or good side of her.[11] Hernández shows the influence of this archetype in his continuous identification of the enemy with the Feminine. He and his comrades are the solar males at war with her. The Hero then attempts to slay the Old Spirit Father, who embodies and defends the society's traditional value system. In a static society, the sons unquestioningly accept the fathers' values. The Hero, however, is called to reject these values, to establish a new covenant or to reveal a new truth. This we see Hernández doing in all those ideological poems constituting Theme 4: the capitalist-fascist system was the Terrible Father.

The presentation of the four "universal concerns" of sex, death, love, and eternal return, the constants in Hernández's work, is different in this period. In the majority of the work sex does not figure at all. It only appears in *Shepherd of Death* and "The Song of the Soldier Spouse," and then it is no longer the lustful coupling of the first period, but a loving, conjugal act which will result in the conception of a child. The peasant plays draw a clear judgmental distinction between lust—both authority figures are satyrs—and sex as an expression of love. Love in this period is principally fraternal. The peasant plays have a conventional love plot, but brotherly love or class solidarity is equally important. The narcissism of the first period has been supplanted. In *The Shepherd of Death*, which has both a love and a war plot, the shepherd's greater love is for his comrades and his country. In the first act and the last Pedro marches off to war, leaving his beloved Ana behind: "Tengo que vengar los muertos / y los vivos tengo que vengar" ("I must avenge the dead / And the living must I avenge," p. 925). Puccini remarks Hernández's profound sense of identification with his brothers during this period, citing a stanza of the poem "Hunger" wherein Hernández gives plaintive witness to his "proletarian essence" (p. 92):

> Ayudadme a ser hombre: no me dejéis ser fiera
> hambrienta, encarnizada, sitiada eternamente.
> Yo, animal familiar, con esta sangre obrera
> os doy la humanidad que mi canción presiente. (p. 327)

> Help me to be human: do not let me be a beast,
> Starving, enraged, eternally cornered.
> I, a family animal, with this worker's blood
> Give to you the humanity which my song prefigures.

Given this humanitarian devotion, it is not surprising, Puccini writes, that references to Hernández's personal life are "extremely rare" or diluted in the collective experience. "Instead 'man,' 'a man,' and 'men' are the palingenetic protagonists of even the most somber poems in the book" (p. 92). Puccini believes that the war was the most important experience in Hernández's life, and consequently in his work, for in the war "Hernández discovers his own dimension, something like an identification of the individual with the collectivity: not only in the encounter of his personal history as a man of primordial emotions with the sorrow of the world (the 'soldier-spouse' is the synthesis and emblem of this encounter), but also in the naturalized and humanized valuation of life" (p. 146).

Death is no longer regarded with melancholy but with joy. Hernández and many of his fellow poets preach that to die for the cause is to live eternally. The dead man will be welcomed into the lap of mother earth, of "Mother Spain," where he will fecundate the land. His country will keep his memory alive, as will his proud family. Death is not only praised in much of this poetry, it is desired, cited as a bull would be cited. Lechner notes that the theme of fecundating death became so common in the war poetry as to constitute a new topos (commonplace, p. 175). But Lechner believes Hernández was an exception among the Republican poets in the use of this topos: "death in [his] war poetry is almost always *the* end, absolute zero, total annihilation; only in three cases is there an example of fecundating death" (p. 163). He then lists the three examples and identifies other poems in which "death is not totally negative, but neither is it deeply fecundating." I find very little difference between the first class of poems and the second, in which, for example, one poem reads:

> Siempre serán famosas
> estas sangres cubiertas de abriles y de mayos,
> que hacen vibrar las dilatadas fosas
> con su vigor que se decide en rayos. (p. 278)

> They will always be famous,
> These bloods covered with Aprils and Mays,
> Which make the vast graves vibrate
> With their vigor which resolves itself in lightning.

Perpetuation through progeny is also mentioned in this period, especially in the "Song of the Soldier Spouse" and the *Shepherd of Death*.

VI *Symbols and Motifs*

The symbols of Hernández's second period are most easily considered according to his own dichotomization: those which represent the Republicans, the revolutionaries, the *machos;* and those which represent the Nationalists, the "females," the cowards, the conservatives. In addition to these symbols there are several which represent the enduring world, backdrop to the ephemeral drama of the war: roses, earth, death, eternal return, the impermanence of man in the timeless world, agriculture (with sexual connotations, as in the first period), and the nature of the "Captive."

The principal symbols or motifs associated with the goodness and masculinity of the Republicans are: spume or foam (they literally foam at the mouth in their eagerness), trees (phallic and bound to the earth), lions, the foot and walking, rivers, blood, wind, war, bulls, light, fig trees, hard work, a death wish, and perpetuity. Many of these symbols were used extensively in the first period, when masculinity was also a major concern. The symbols and motifs associated with the enemy are equally familiar, for they are the ones Hernández used to denote the Great Mother in earlier work: beasts or wild animals, spiders, dogs (which are cowardly); oxen, containers of various sorts, cloven hooves and claws, rocks, the moon, shadows, dust, calm or repose, and laziness.

Several symbols—arms and hands, blood, and water—change meaning according to the adjective applied to them. They can be positive or negative, as in "The Hands":

> Dos especies de manos se enfrentan en la vida,
> brotan del corazón, irrumpen por los brazos, ·
> . . . .
> La mano es la herramienta del alma, su mensaje,
> y el cuerpo tiene en ella su rama combatiente.
> Alzad, moved las manos en un gran oleaje,
> hombres de mi simiente.
>
> Ante la aurora veo surgir las manos puras
> de los trabajadores terrestres y marinos,
> . . . .
> Estas sonoras manos oscuras y lucientes,
> las reviste una piel de invencible corteza,
> y son inagotables y generosas fuentes
> de vida y de riqueza.

Como si con los astros el polvo peleara,
como si los planetas lucharan con gusanos,
la especie de las manos trabajadora y clara
lucha con otras manos.

Feroces y reunidas en un bando sangriento,
avanzan al hundirse los cielos vespertinos
unas manos de hueso lívido y avariento,
paisaje de asesinos. (pp. 294–95)

Two species of hands confront each other in life,
They sprout from the heart, erupt from the arms.
. . . .
The hand is the soul's tool, its message,
And in it the body finds its fighting branch.
Raise, move your hands in a great wave,
Men of my seed.

Before the dawn I see the surge of the pure hands
Of the workers of the earth and the sea.
. . . .
These sonorous hands dark and shining
Are covered with a skin of invincible cortex,
And they are inexhaustible and generous founts
Of life and wealth.

As if the dust were to struggle with the stars,
As if the planets were to battle with worms,
The species of hands that is hard-working and bright
Battles with other hands.

Ferocious and grouped in bloody bands,
There advance—with the sinking of the vespertine skies—
Some hands of livid and avaricious bone,
Landscape of assassins.

We can see several other symbols in this poem (including various
stanzas which I have omitted) which exemplify our earlier list. The
Republicans, represented synecdochally by their hands (each side
had a characteristic salute, which makes the equation of hands with
classes of people easily comprehensible), are "hard-working,"
"pure," associated with the dawn, and the spring, with stars and the

planets; they are "bright," "shining," constructive, aggressive; they
are fountains, they are noisy, sonorous. The Nationalists are depicted stanza by stanza as the Republicans' antitheses: they are dust
(not fountains), worms; they are twice associated with nightfall; they
are lazy, avaricious (not generous), destructive or passive; they are
silent ("They haven't sounded: they don't sing. Their fingers wander
hoarse . . ."), they clutch daggers and chalices and crimes and
death.

There are relatively few symbols which are exclusive to this
period, as we might expect from Hernández's professed desire to
simplify his work. Lions and dogs, war and the death wish are the
only significant new ones. Lions symbolize the strength and masculinity of the Republicans:[12]

> Los bueyes doblan la frente,
> impotentemente mansa,
> delante de los castigos:
> los leones la levantan
> y al mismo tiempo castigan
> con su clamorosa zarpa. (p. 270)

> The oxen lower their heads,
> Impotently tame,
> In the face of punishment:
> Lions raise their heads
> And simultaneously punish
> With their clamorous claw.
>   . . .

> Han muerto como mueren los leones:
> peleando y rugiendo,
> espumosa la boca de canciones,
> de ímpetu las cabezas y las venas de estruendo. (p. 278)

> They have died like lions die
> Fighting and roaring,
> Mouths frothy with songs,
> Heads [frothy] with momentum, and veins with tumult.

Noisiness is a masculine attribute which contrasts with the passive
silence of the Feminine. Note that the Nationalists are compared to
oxen, or castrated bulls, in the first fragment.

In a late poem, "Hunger," which reflects Miguel's lessening ardor
for war, we see a change in his evaluation of lions and other fierce
animals. Whereas at first they symbolized a praiseworthy ferocity,
now they symbolize the growing bestialization of his hungry countrymen:

El animal influye sobre mí con extremo,
la fiera late en todas mis fuerzas, mis pasiones.
A veces he de hacer un esfuerzo supremo
para callar en mí la voz de los leones.
. . . .
Por hambre vuelve el hombre sobre los laberintos
donde la vida habita siniestramente sola.
Reaparece la fiera, recobra sus instintos,
sus patas erizadas, sus rencores, su cola.
. . . .
regresa a la pezuña, retrocede al dominio
del colmillo, y avanza sobre los comedores.
. . . .
Entonces sólo veo sobre el mundo una piara
de tigres, y en mis ojos la visión duele y pesa.

Yo no tengo en el alma tanto tigre admitido,
tanto chacal prohijado, . . .
. . . .
Ayudadme a ser hombre: no me degéis ser fiera. (pp. 326–27)

The animal holds great sway over me,
The beast howls beneath all my forces, my passions.
At times I must make a supreme effort
To silence in myself the voice of the lion.
. . . .
Hunger impels man to return to the labyrinths
Where life lives sinister and solitary.
The beast reappears, recovers its instincts,
Its bristling paws, its rancors, its tail.
. . . .
He returns to the cloven hoof, he regresses to the dominion
Of the fang, and he advances upon the eating places.
. . . .
Then I see over the world only a troop
Of tigers, and in my eyes the sight aches and depresses.

I have not admitted so much tiger in my soul

Nor adopted so much jackal, . . .
. . . .
Help me to be human: do not let me be a wild animal.

Dogs, jackals, and hares are natural choices to symbolize the enemy. To call anyone a dog is to insult him, a jackal even more so. "Liebre" (hare) is a colloquial term for coward in Spanish. The dog and the hare are both associated with the Feminine archetype: the hare is a fertility symbol (Neumann, *The Great Mother*, p. 141 n.), the dog the Terrible Mother's "principal animal, the howler by night, and the finder of tracks . . ., the companion of the dead" (Neumann, *The Great Mother*, p. 170). Hernández calls the Nationalists these names and more in the Quevedesque "The Cowards":

> En el corazón son liebres,
> gallinas en las entrañas,
> galgos de rápido vientre,
> que en épocas de paz ladran
> y en épocas de cañones
> desaparecen del mapa.
> . . . .
> ¿Dónde iréis que no vayáis
> a la muerte, liebres pálidas,
> podencos de poca fe
> y de demasiadas patas?
> . . . .
> . . .vais del sol a la sombra
> llenos de desconfianza. (pp. 274–75)

> In the heart they are hares,
> Chickens in the guts.
> Greyhounds with rapid bellies,
> Which in peacetime bark
> And in cannontime
> Disappear from the map.
> . . . .
> Where will you go that is not
> To death, pallid hares,
> Hounds of little faith
> And of too many paws?
> . . . .
> . . .you go from the sun to the shadow
> Full of mistrust.

For Hernández the war had a larger significance than its daily, tangible reality. Combat became symbolic of a greater battle of discord in many spheres, hence it is rarely described realistically. It is magnified (in part to encourage the combatants) to cosmic proportions and described in sidereal terms, moral terms, sexual terms. It is pre–eminently the hero's proving ground, his struggle against the World Parents.

> Sobre la piel del cielo, sobre sus precipicios,
> se remontan los hombres. ¿Quién ha impulsado el vuelo?
> Sonoros, derramados en aéreos ejercicios,
> raptan la piel del cielo.
> . . . .
> En un avance cósmico de llamas y zumbidos
> que aeródromos de pueblos emocionados lanzan,
> los soldados del aire, veloces, esculpidos,
> acerados avanzan.
>
> El azul se enardece y adquiere una alegría,
> un movimiento, una juventud libre y clara,
> lo mismo que si mayo, la claridad del día
> corriera, resonara. (pp. 323–24)
>
> Over the skin of the sky, over its precipices,
> The men soar. Who has impelled their flight?
> Sonorous, spread out in airborn exercises,
> They ravish the skin of the sky.
> . . . .
> In a cosmic advance of flames and hums
> Which airdromes of fervent peoples launch,
> The soldiers of the air, swift, sculpted,
> Steely advance.
>
> The blue catches fire and gains a joy,
> A movement, a youth free and bright,
> Just as if May, the brightness of the day
> Were racing, resounding.
>   . . .
> Subes conmigo, vas de cumbre en cumbre,
> mientras tus hijos, mis hermanos, ruedan
> como ganaderías de indestructible lumbre,
> de torres y cristales:
> de potros que descienden y se quedan,

chocándose, volcándose, suspensos
de varios precipicios celestiales,
el relincho a torrentes y los brazos inmensos. (p. 348)

[Spain], You rise with me, you go from peak to peak,
While your sons, my brothers, roll along
Like ranches of indestructible fire,
Of towers and glass,
Of colts which descend and remain,
Clashing, overturning, suspended
From various celestial precipices,
Their cries of joy torrential, their arms immense.

In the final scene of *The Shepherd of Death* Hernández portrays the triumph of the Loyalists (Republicans):

(. . . The black stain will have disappeared from the map of Spain and the black soldiers from the stage; there will remain a group of soldiers, illuminated by the light of blood and of the full-blown midday. . . .)

Paso a paso, mi tierra vuelve a mí. Trozo a trozo,
vuelven la claridad del día y el centeno.
. . . .
Por una madrugada de gallos iracundos,
un ejército joven como las madrugadas
conquista, paso a paso, los arados profundos,
los pueblos invadidos, los hijos, las azadas.

Soplan los toros y hacen temblar la luz del cielo:
los hombres que yo digo la aumentan y la aclaran,
. . . .
Haciendo luz la luz y luz la sombra densa,
van los padres del sol, los padres del granito,
que hacen la espiga grande, y hacen la vida inmensa,
y el vientre de las madres poblado de infinito. (p. 927)

Step by step, my land returns to me. Bit by bit,
The day's brightness and the rye return.
. . . .
Through a dawn of wrathful roosters
An army as young as the dawn
Conquers, step by step, the deep plowings,
The occupied villages, the children, the hoes.

The bulls blow and they make the light in the sky tremble:
The men of whom I speak increase and clarify it.
. . . .

Making light the light and light the dense shadow,
The fathers of the sun advance, the fathers of granite,
Who make the spike large, who make life immense,
And who people with infinity the wombs of the mothers.

Repeatedly, battles are portrayed as light conquering the darkness, as we see in the previous fragments, or in this speech from
Shepherd of Death, where the loyal Cuban castigates an enemy:

Bien calificados vamos
con el color diferente
que nos han calificado:
rojo y blanco. . . .
. . . .

Rojo yo como la vida,
blanco tú como la muerte.
Yo del color de la sangre,
tú del color de la especie
de lo frío, de lo muerto,
ni cal, ni espuma, ni nieve.
Una noche muerta y blanca
frente a un día rojo y verde. (pp. 866–67)
We are well characterized
By the different colors
They have assigned us:
Red and white. . . .
. . . .

I am red like life,
You are white like death.
I, the color of blood,
You, the color of the species
That are cold, dead,
Neither lime, nor spume, nor snow.
A night dead and white
Facing a day red and green.

Another motif which figures importantly in Hernández's war production is that of the body and its will as the best weapons, superior
to the impersonal weaponry of the Nationalists. Clearly, such a
contention is wholly irrational: the Republicans were being deci-
mated for lack of weapons. Why then would Hernández lie about

this lack, say that it was militarily inconsequential? Like the praise-of-death motif which so markedly contradicts Hernández's sensual and intellectual love of life, the motif of hands vs. guns (or men vs. machines, as Berns denominates it) is symptomatic of his willingness to surrender everything—reason, truth, deeply held belief—to the Republican cause. Berns notes that in the war collections Hernández depends on bodily images "which are presented in a surrealistically distorted fashion that conveys the pain and horror of the situation" (p. 97). "In opposition to the totally impersonal force which leaves no traces of what it destroys, Miguel Hernández constantly has parts of the body serve as both offensive and defensive weapons. In the face of obliteration, man will fight with what is most integral to him . . ." (p. 101). Thus we can see that Hernández's early physicality has continued in this poetry, but that it has been so subordinated to his new cause as to have been radically transformed. His body is important now because it is a weapon, not because it is his means of experiencing life. The phantasmagoric poem "El herido" ("The Wounded Man," pp. 328–29) illustrates this new valuation of the body:

> Herido estoy, miradme: necesito más vidas.
> La que contengo es poca para el gran cometido
> de sangre que quisiera perder por las heridas.
> . . . .
> Para la libertad sangro, lucho, pervivo.
> Para la libertad, mis ojos y mis manos,
> como un árbol carnal, generoso y cautivo,
> doy a los cirujanos.
> . . . .
> Para la libertad me desprendo a balazos
> de los que han revolcado su estatua por el lodo.
> Y me desprendo a golpes de mis pies, de mis brazos,
> de mi casa, de todo. (pp. 328–29)

> I am wounded: look at me. I need more lives.
> The one I possess is not enough for the great commission
> Of blood that I should like to lose from my wounds.
> . . . .
> For liberty I bleed, I fight, I survive.
> For liberty, my eyes and my hands,
> Like a tree of flesh, generous and captive,
> I give to the surgeons.
> . . . .

For liberty I sever myself with bullets
From those who have trampled on its statue in the mud.
And I sever myself with blows from my feet, from my hands,
From my house, from everything.

The exaltation of men over machines was widespread in Spanish
committed poetry, Lechner writes. It was tied in with the exaltation
of the farm—not the industrial—worker as the ideal proletarian;
with the traditional "disdain for the city and praise for the country";
with the peculiarly Spanish identification of the machine with the
bourgeoisie, which resulted in the socialist's condemnation of one
with the other. (Lechner imputes these unique attitudes to the
tardiness of Spain's industrialization, and to the fact that the country
was still so heavily agricultural at the time of the war [I, 128–29].)
    Gradually the political zeal which had sustained Hernández in the
early years of the war diminished. In the last poems of the period a
new motif emerges: the search for a new truth, for fresh values. He
had won the psychological battle he had been waging against powerful enemies to constitute himself as an individual. The Captive—his
creative unconscious as well as a flesh-and-blood spouse—could now
help him in his quest for a sustaining truth, for what is called in
archetypal terms the "Treasure." Joseph Campbell in *The Hero of a
Thousand Faces* calls this truth the "Ultimate Boon": it is in part the
ability to perceive that man's most important values are the inner
ones. At this point in his life, with the war degenerating all around
him, Hernández has not achieved any such clear insight: he only
knows that his old truth—war and politics—no longer commands his
allegiance. In "First Song," partially cited above (p. 94), Hernández
laments that the world is out of joint, that men are behaving so
bestially that killing one's own child is a possibility:

            El animal que canta:
            el animal que puede
            llorar y echar raíces,
            rememoró sus garras.

            Garras que revestía
            de suavidad y flores,
            pero que, al fin, desnuda
            en toda su crueldad.

Crepitan en mis manos.
Aparta de ellas, hijo.
Estoy dispuesto a hundirlas,
dispuesto a proyectarlas
sobre tu carne leve.

He regresado al tigre.
Aparta o te destrozo. (p. 315)

The animal that sings:
The animal that can
Cry and put down roots,
Remembered his claws.

Claws that he disguised
With gentleness and flowers,
But which, in the end, he unsheaths
In all their cruelty.

They crackle on my hands.
Get away from them, son.
I am prepared to sink them,
Prepared to project them
Onto your delicate flesh.

I have returned to the tiger.
Get away or I will destroy you.

Both in the "Last Song" (cited in full on pp. 88–89) and in the Dedication of *Man the Spy to* Neruda (cited in part on p. 78), we see evidence of Hernández's searching for a new truth to direct his life. He has begun to suspect that it is love, not politics, which can transform the future: he has begun to turn inward once again.

We have already characterized the tone of this work as propagandistic, hyperbolic, precipitate. For Lechner, Hernández's committed poetry differs from that of his fellows (from Prados and from Alberti, principally) in that it is far more aggressive and combative. He tentatively attributes this to Hernández's humbler social origins (which gave him more of a vested interest in the triumph of the proletariat), to all the years in which he went hungry, to the poverty and injustices suffered by his family. "More combative and at first glance more optimistic than the poetry of Alberti, [Hernández's work] is actually more desolating in its totality" (p. 163).

Puccini describes the stylistic elements which give this poetry its characteristically overwrought, exalted tone. After citing a number of instances when Hernández, impelled by his "singular participation," interrupts the orderly development of his poems to interject a hortatory plea or an autobiographical reference, or to change the addressee, Puccini summarizes: "Corresponding to this mixing of tones, to this violent alternation of epic, elegiac, autobiographical, vocative, monitory and imprecatory lines, to this subterranean fusion of the various degrees of the poet's participation in the material sung, is the mixing, the alternation and the fusion of distinct planes of language," for example, the language of the old ballad books; of the epic ballads (cantares de gesta); the stylized language of the Golden Age classics; the plebian language of anger and sarcasm, with its clichés; and finally the "iterative, synaesthetic, visionary" language of Surrealism (p. 82).

VII   Analysis of Theatrical Works

Since we have already cited most of the prose written in this period for its content, and since it is not literary in any real sense of the term, we shall omit it here. Relatively brief consideration will be given the wartime dramatic works. Concha Zardoya has observed that "critics and friends alike coincide in scorning or deflating the dramatic talent of Miguel Hernández, or, at best, they judge the lyric poet to be far superior to the playwright" (p. 696). She does not agree with this evaluation, but an objective critic must, for while Hernández may have had a "tragic sense," and a personal "dramatism," as she says, he never succeeded in translating them into a convincing play. We shall not dwell overlong on his drama here, then, in spite of its quantitative importance in the period.

The four plays divide into several categories, as we have previously said: Sons of Stone and The Comeliest Peasant are peasant plays; Wartime Theater is propaganda, and as such outside our consideration; The Shepherd of Death is a combination peasant/propaganda play.

Both Sons of Stone and The Comeliest Peasant are modeled to some extent after Lope de Vega's Fuenteovejuna and Peribáñez.[13] Each deals with a despotic landowner who abuses his workers in a variety of ways. In *Sons of Stone* he lowers the miners' wages (to finance his debauchery) and demands more work; the miners stage a hunger strike to which he retaliates by closing down the mines. Meanwhile, he has been pursuing the beautiful Retama, who becomes the Shepherd's (common-law) wife. To eliminate the Shepherd, the Señor sends an overseer out to kill his sheep, whereupon the Shepherd kills the overseer and is imprisoned. The Señor then rapes Retama, despite her advanced stage of pregnancy. This final violation of "hacienda y honor" (property and honor) sparks the uprising against the landowner, just as Laurencia's rape did in *Fuenteovejuna*. The Shepherd returns to find Retama, who has aborted the child because of the violation, at the point of death. He incites the miners to insurrection. In the final scene the Civil Guards massacre the hapless but unrepentant townspeople.

In *The Comeliest Peasant* all of the farm workers except Juan, the comeliest (the Spanish title *El labrador de más aire* can also be translated "the most enterprising peasant"), accept the landowner Don Augusto's demands for a higher share of their yield. Juan tries to organize his fellows to rebel but is unsuccessful. Meanwhile, Don Augusto has been lusting after Encarnación, Juan's cousin (who is secretly in love with Juan). Augusto assaults her and Juan—like Frondoso in *Fuenteovejuna*—comes to her aid, humiliating Don Augusto, who vows revenge. The enraged lord buys an assassin (a young man who had always envied Juan), who sets upon Juan with a sickle. Juan dies in the lap of his cousin Encarnación with whom (he has finally realized after a dalliance with Don Augusto's daughter) he is truly in love.

Hernández later called both of these plays dramas in "exaltation of labor and condemnation of the bourgeoisie," but when they were written they were certainly intended to present modern variations on the basic *comedia* theme of the peasant's honor vs. the gentleman's depravity. Like Lope's *Fuenteovejuna* (*Sons of Stone* is set in a town called Montecabra, Goat Hill, an obvious imitation of *Fuenteovejuna*, Sheep Spring), *Sons of Stone* is based on historical fact, the uprising of the Asturian miners in October, 1934. Guerrero Zamora points out other Lopean influences on the two works, especially in the lack of detailed characterization (pp. 404–07): "all of the characters in *Sons* and *Peasant* act out their [part in the] plot, not their psychology; they are functioning pieces of the theme." He divides all of these "block figures" into the following categories:

1. Characters who represent tyranny
2. Characters who represent humble honesty, some of whom
   a. revolt
   b. resign themselves
   c. sell out
3. Characters who represent love (p. 407)

Ruíz Ramón feels that Miguel's one-dimensional characters are not Lopean but melodramatic, not universal but trivially idiosyncratic (p. 313). *Sons of Stone* and *The Comeliest Peasant* share many structural and stylistic features. Both have three acts, the first divided into two *cuadros* (we see Lorca's influence in this designation of scenes as "frames" or "pictures") or *fases* (phases); the second and third into three. In *Sons of Stone* the acts are subtitled "Summer," "Autumn," and "Winter." "Winter" being the last act immediately suggests that the play will end tragically.

Sons of Stone has two plots: social or political, and amorous. They are intertwined and developed with a precision that is almost mathematical. In Act I, for example, we find the following structure. First phase: Scenes i–v present the social situation; Scene vi introduces a complication, the death of the beloved landlord; Scene vii introduces the amorous plot. Next phase: Scenes i–iv present the changed social situation under the new landlord; Scenes v–vi the new amorous situation; Scene vii another complication: the landlord vows revenge on the Shepherd; Scene viii, life and nature continue unchanged.

There is one "extra" scene in the second phase, representing the symbolic intrusion of the new landlord. Otherwise the phases are mirror images of each other. Acts II and III are equally meticulous. "The schematism of *Sons* is overcome in *Peasant*," Puccini writes, "thanks especially to a less rigid distribution of the dramatic effects and movements and to a richer, more spontaneous articulation of the characters. . . . Lacking real dialogues, or open and dynamic scenic contrasts, the play is composed of a lovely checkerboard of touching 'confessions' which the principal characters, closed and almost immobile in their own feelings, *recite* like *themes* of a delicate symphony or a sustained ballet" (p. 69).

The Comeliest Peasant has three plots: the social (the villagers' interactions), the political (the landowner vs. the serfs), and the

amorous (Juan and Encarnación; all the young people), which Hernández combines and alternates very freely. On the negative side
this spontaneity results in a number of dramatically superfluous
characters (Antonina, Carmelo, Tomás) and equally superfluous
scenes. One is not surprised to discover that the play is almost twice
as long as the typical Golden Age peasant play.

The Shepherd of Death is an exemplary play, so its organization is
quite different from the previous two. In the first act the form is one
of concentric or converging circles which progressively individualize
and locate the Shepherd, Pedro. First his village is dramatized, then
his home and family, then his relationship with his fiancée. He is
both universalized—for all young men live within similar social
frames—and particularized, since the convergence of the specific
frames Hernández has chosen eventually excludes all young men
other than Pedro. In the first act all of those forces which would
thwart the young man's push for independence seek to prevent
Pedro from going off to war. His fiancée Ana tries to hold him with
the sexual favors she has previously denied him, but he will not be
swayed.

Act II has a contrapuntal structure. Not only are there two
settings—the trenches of the Guadarrama and the besieged city of
Madrid—but the action in each setting is double. In the trenches
the Republican soldiers speak, sing, and philosophize about the
noble aims of their war, about the need for bravery, etc. There are
various contrasts to this essentially passive idealism: one of the soldiers is killed by a sniper; a voice from the Nationalist side debates
with them; and finally, Pedro goes off to capture an enemy machine
gun, putting the ideals of war—bravery, heroism, self-sacrifice—
into practice. The action in Madrid is antiphonal. First there enters
a mother grieving and raving over the death of her infant in a
bombing raid. She is followed by a group of "Undesirables" whose
self-serving complaints and plans to desert Madrid contrast sharply
with her continuing loyalty to the cause which has cost her everything.

Act III presents another exemplary contrast between brave men
(Pedro and the Cuban) who go out to help their captured Major and
some murmurers who stay behind and try to convince the loyal that
the Major has defected. The Major dies bravely at the hands of the
savage Moorish troops, and Pedro and the Cuban carry his body

back to the trenches, where they prop it up—like the Cid's dead body—to encourage and inspire the troops. The final scene is of battle, when once again the Loyalists repulse the enemy.

Act IV shows the soldiers at rest. They have given Pedro a nickname—Shepherd of Death—for his bravery. He receives a letter from Ana, who begs him to come home for the birth of their child. He returns to the village briefly to deliver his dead comrades' effects to their families, to kiss his son, to remind his family and the village that their cause is not yet won. He marches off. This act forms a frame with the first, for both show the individual soldier, show how his commitment affects his woman, his family, his village. The middle acts are more abstract and propagandistic: in them Pedro is one soldier among many. The final scene in Act IV is a poetic coda, delivered by the Voice of the Poet (see pp. 105–06)

Sons of Stone is a prose drama, whereas the other two are in verse, but there is little difference among the three in vocabulary and syntax. All three use figurative language, *The Comeliest Peasant* far more so than the other two. Guerrero Zamora notes the frequent use of parallelisms, of correlations and other reiterative formulas typical of classical poetry, as well as popular parallelistic recourses such as refrains, throughout *Peasant* (pp. 407–17).

The themes which predominate in *Sons of Stone* are: (1) the inherent honor or integrity of the peasant contrasted to the villainy of the gentleman, a stock Golden Age theme; (2) the passivity of the masses (symbolized by that most passive of protests, the hunger strike), who need a catalytic agent—a hero—to incite them to rebellion; (3) man's injustice, which is more powerful than rightfulness or Nature (all the townspeople are killed for their attempt to redress the landowner's wrongs. In *Fuenteovejuna*, the peasants were vindicated by the monarchs). In the elaboration of the first theme we see the glimmerings of Hernández's tendency to overstatement or hyperbole during the period, for surely no laborers have ever been so devoted to the pure joy of work as these miners, nor has any landlord every been so gratuitously evil as the Señor.

This theme of the peasants' honor also illustrates why *Sons of Stone* is transitional. It is certainly a topos borrowed from the Golden Age, as were so many themes in the first period, yet Hernández has refurbished it with contemporary political overtones that make it a perfect expression of his new *engagée* philosophy. He still seems to accept the inherent rightness of a lord / peasant hierzrchy in society, so long as that lord is a just one. By the time he wrote *The Comeliest Peasant*, approximately one year later, he had rejected that belief. Juan is an egalitarian, a communist:

DON AUGUSTO: I am the owner of the village.
JUAN: You may be the owner of whatever,
     But you do not own me. (p. 715)

ISABEL   We are of different castes:
[Augusto's daughter]: You are a man without a name . . .
                   You are no more than a laborer.
JUAN: Nor less.
ISABEL: You are not enough.
JUAN: It is my greatest pride
     To be a laborer. (p. 738)

In *Wartime Theater* and *Shepherd* the only distinctions left between men are those between enemy and friend, coward and hero.

The second theme in *Sons of Stone*, the need for a hero to galvanize the passive masses, is an archetypal one, giving the play a note of universality to balance the topicality of its politics. Again and again the laborers are characterized as passive, lambs waiting for a shepherd. They call frequently and futilely on Nature to help them. By the end of the play it has become clear that man can only look to other men for help, that neither from God nor Nature is aid forthcoming.

SHEPHERD: . . . But how can you go on like this, banded together like a
          cowardly flock attacked by a wolf? In what meek womb were
          you engendered?
FIRST MINER: The rock bore us, the rock has sustained us, in the rock we live
          and beneath the rock we will surely die without having raised a
          single arm against the one who mistreats us. (p. 655).

They are too much in the stone's power, in the Great Mother's power, to break away. The Shepherd is the lightning bolt they had clamored for, the "wind which came to fan the flame" ("Viento ha sido el pastor que vino a soplar el fuego," p. 660). Miguel obviously identified with the hero whom he made a shepherd like himself. We know that he explicitly identified himself with Juan in *The Comeliest Peasant* (see p. 71), who like the Shepherd tried—although unsuccessfully—to spark a revolt. And finally, Pedro in *The*

Shepherd of Death is another heroic figure with a great deal of Miguel Hernández in him. Even in the waning months of the war, then, Hernández identified himself with the archetypal hero. The third important theme in *Sons of Stone* is a pessimistic one: man's injustice will triumph. This is an implicit rejection of the Christian message, just as Theme 2 is. Man must establish his own order on earth, with no supernatural help.

The major themes of *Peasant* and *Shepherd* are similar to those of *Sons of Stone*. Both deal with the heroic role of breaking away from the old and inaugurating the new. In *Peasant* the old is represented by the nearly feudal landholding system; in *Shepherd* by the intense conservatism and overprotectiveness of Pedro's milieu. *The Comeliest Peasant* is as pessimistic as *Sons of Stone*, for in the end Juan is killed by a petty rival before he can fulfill his destiny. *The Shepherd of Death* is a tendentious play in which there is no room for petty bourgeois sentiments like pessimism. Even if in the final act Pedro is marching off to death, his life will not have been in vain. All three plays are unsparing in their criticism of greed and selfishness. Hernández's ideal of human behavior was unselfishness and altruism, which he saw threatened on all sides. Lust and cowardice are related vices: one is greed for another's body, the other a manifestation of egoism. The villains in the plays are without exception characterized by these sins of the overreaching self.

VIII *Poetry*

We shall analyze one poem from each collection of war poetry. From *Wind of the People:*

El niño yuntero

Carne de yugo, ha nacido
más humillado que bello,
con el cuello perseguido
por el yugo para el cuello.

Nace, como la herramienta,
a los golpes destinado,
de una tierra descontenta
y un insatisfecho arado.

Entre estiércol puro y vivo
de vacas, trae a la vida
un alma color de olivo
vieja ya y encallecida.

Empieza a vivir, y empieza
a morir de punta a punta
levantando la corteza
de su madre con la yunta.
. . . .
Cada nuevo día es
más raíz, menos criatura,
que escucha bajo sus pies
la voz de la sepultura.

Y como raíz se hunde
en la tierra lentamente
para que la tierra inunde
de paz y panes su frente.

Me duele este niño hambriento
como una grandiosa espina,
y su vivir ceniciento
revuelve mi alma de encina.
. . . .
¿Quién salvará a este chiquillo
menor que un grano de avena?
¿De dónde saldrá el martillo
verdugo de esta cadena?

Que salga del corazón
de los hombres journaleros,
que antes de ser hombres son
y han sido niños yunteros. (pp. 272–74)

The Plowboy

Flesh of yoke, he is born
More humiliated than handsome,
With his neck hunted down
By a yoke for the neck.

He is born, like a tool,
To be destined to blows,
Out of an unhappy land
By an unsatisfied plow.

Among cow dung, sharp
And pure, he brings to life
A soul the color of olives,
Old already, and calloused.

He begins to live, and begins
To die from head to toe
Raising the crust
Of his mother with the yoke.
. . . .
Each new day finds him
More root, less creature,
Hearing beneath his feet
The call of the sepulchre.

And like a root he sinks
Slowly into the earth
So that the earth might flood
His brow with bread and peace.

This starving child hurts me
Like an enormous thorn,
And his ashen existence
Shakes my soul of oak.
. . . .
Who will save this little boy
Smaller than a grain of oats?
Whence will come the hammer
To be executioner of this chain?

Let it come from the hearts
Of day-laboring men
Who before they are men are
And have been children of the plow.

The poem is composed of fifteen *cuartetas*, octosyllabic quatrains
rhyming *abab*. The effect of full rhyme (rather than the subtler
assonance) in combination with the short octosyllable is a singsong

poem, which "The Plowboy" certainly is. Hernández has com-
pounded this effect by alliteration and anaphora, as we can see in
the first stanza. The words "yugo," "humillado," "bello," and
"cuello" all contain the closely related (especially in uncultured Cas-
tilian) *y* and *ll* sounds; the words "yugo" and "cuello" are repeated in
full, not felicitously in such a short stanza. Guerrero Zamora judges
this stanza to be "not just cacophonous, but padded out, with a
second verse that presents a comparison . . . between absurd
terms" (p. 277). In the third stanza the *v* is repeated six times; in
stanza 4 the first verse is an example of epanadiplosis, for "empieza"
both begins and ends the line (there is another instance of this trope
in a verse which we have not quoted); the next stanza (not quoted)
begins with "empieza" as well. Other forms of repetition or parallelism abound; a few examples will suggest the variety. Parallelism
or correlations: "por el yugo para el cuello," which can be represented A (preposition)$_1$ B (noun)$_1$ A$_2$ B$_2$; "de una tierra descontenta / y un insatisfecho arado," B$_1$C (adjective)$_1$/C$_2$B$_2$; the use of
several words in close proximity which are derived from the same
root: vivo-vida, sentir-siente, fuerza-fuerte, ser-son-han sido. Yet in
spite of the variety of structuring formulas Hernández has used, this
is a sloppy poem. The repetitions are monotonous because they are
mechanical. They do not grow out of the content of the poem, unless
we agree with Berns's suggestion that the language of the war
poetry, with its constant use of repetition, creates "a sense of bar-
renness of language to match and describe that of the land" (p. 97).

There are essentially three sections to this poem, as Daniel Williams has pointed out (p. 165): the first describes the plowboy and
his hopeless existence; the second relates Hernández's reaction to
the child; the third poses a rhetorical question to Hernández's listeners, which he then answers by giving a command. This change
from description to reaction to interrogation to injunction is typical
of the war poetry, as is the mixture of tones from pathos to pity to
outrage to decisiveness. Puccini credits most of these "ruptures" to
the special requirements of a poetry which was to be recited (p. 84).
Certainly most of the repetitiousness in the diction can also be
ascribed to the exigencies of oral poetry (which does not make them
any less monotonous, to be sure, or any more aesthetic).

The images which Hernández uses to describe the plowboy vary
greatly but do not seem to have an organic development. His flesh is
of the yoke; his neck is hunted down by a yoke; he is born from the

womb of the earth like a tool; these are rather fanciful images, surrealistic or irrational. The image of the boy as root sinking deeper into the soil is a striking one, as is the vision of his soul as an old withered olive. But roots do not have ears to listen to imaginary voices, nor do they have foreheads. An inundation of the earth's peace would probably be death, which would preclude a need for bread. And so on. There are far too many logical errors in this poem, just as there are too many infelicitous images: the child like a grandiose thorn, a hammer as an executioner (this may well refer to the Communist symbol of the hammer and sickle); and clichés: "from head to toe," "life is a battle," "sweat is a heavy crown of salt" (in stanzas not quoted), "smaller than a grain of oats." Yet several critics rate "The Plowboy" as one of the most compelling of the poems in *Wind of the People* (see Vivanco, p. 550; Zardoya, p. 670; and José María Balcells, *Miguel Hernández, corazón desmesurado* [Barcelona: Dirosa, 1975], pp. 171–72). As is so frequently the case with Hernández, the critics allow autobiographical elements and the "sincerity" of his message to influence their judgment. Yet while this is conceptually a moving subject, and no one can doubt Hernández's depth of feeling, "The Plowboy" is a mediocre poem. Both by virtue of its passionate conviction and its aesthetic mediocrity, it is representative of *Wind of the People*.

Far more interesting poetically, "July 18, 1936–July 18, 1938" (the first date is the day the war began) gives poignant testimony to the changes two years of war have wrought in Hernández. The zeal which had inspired and maintained him through those early months is no longer sufficient. In this poem he laments the loss of life which he had exalted in such earlier poems as "Nuestra juventud no muere" ("Our Youth Does Not Die"), "Sitting on the Dead," "Elegía segunda" ("Second Elegy"), and "Llamo a la juventud" ("I Call the Youth").

> Es sangre, no granizo, lo que azota mis sienes.
> Son dos años de sangre: son dos inundaciones.
> Sangre de acción solar, devoradora vienes,
> hasta dejar sin nadie y ahogados los balcones.
>
> Sangre que es el mejor de los mejores bienes.
> Sangre que atesoraba para el amor sus dones.
> Vedla enturbiando mares, sobrecogiendo trenes,
> desalentando toros donde alentó leones.

El tiempo es sangre. El tiempo circula por mis venas.
Y ante el reloj y el alba me siento más que herido,
y oigo un chocar de sangres de todos los tamaños.

Sangre donde se puede bañar la muerte apenas:
fulgor emocionante que no ha palidecido,
porque lo recogieron mis ojos de mil años. (p. 339)

It is blood, not hail, which beats down on my temples.
It is two years of blood: it is two inundations.
Blood of solar action, you come ravening,
Until you leave the balconies deserted and drowned.

Blood which is the best of our best goods.
Blood which used to treasure its gifts for love.
Look at it roiling seas, overtaking trains,
Discouraging bulls where it once encouraged lions.

Time is blood. Time circulates in my veins.
And before the clock and the dawn I feel myself more than wounded,
And I hear a collision of bloods of every size.

Blood in which one can scarcely bathe death:
A stirring splendor which has not paled,
Because it was caught by my millenarian eyes.

"July 18" is one of only two sonnets which Hernández wrote during the war (the other is "To the International Soldier Fallen in Spain"). They are unlike the classical hendecasyllabic sonnets of the first period, however, for their verses are alexandrines, the line Hernández so favored in his war poetry. Each verse is divided into hemistiches.

The vocabulary is restrained and simple; there is neither vulgarity nor topical war terminology, nor clichés. The syntax shows the characteristic flexibility of the war period, with several changes of subject and mood in the verbs: (1) "It is blood . . . which beats down"; (2) "Blood . . . , you come ravening"; (3) "Look at it roiling seas." The poem begins as a descriptive third-person narration and ends in the first person, just as "The Plowboy" does. Compared with the stylized diction of the first period, "July 18" is quite discoursive. Yet it escapes the prosaic tone which afflicts many contemporaneous works by virtue of being elliptical and because it is "symbolic."

(Committed artists and "impure" poets alike had explicitly rejected Symbolism for being a movement directed at an educated minority; it was elitist and decadent.) The great symbol of this poem is of course blood, which Hernández develops in a highly personal (non-proletarian) way.

The figures of speech which stand out in "July 18" are apostrophe: to blood, and to his listeners; synecdoche: blood representing men, his eyes representing him; metonymy: the clock representing time; hyperbole: the first stanza; and anaphora: "it is two . . . it is two," "blood which . . . / Blood which . . . ," "Time is blood. Time. . . ." There are four ideas developed in this sonnet, one in each stanza. The first is the wastefulness of so many lives lost, an idea which would have been unthinkable in *Wind of the People*. The second is that war subverts our natural instincts, a theme which becomes the basis of his search for a new truth. In the third stanza Hernández considers the idea that each war casualty presages and brings him closer to his own death, that the bell tolls for him: ". . . before the clock and the dawn I feel myself more than wounded." The fourth stanza provides a halfhearted repudiation of the other three. Hernández repeats one of his standard ideas, that the patriot never dies. But in this case it is not the mothers and girlfriends of the soldiers nor yet their grateful countrymen who will keep their memory green, but the poet, with his "millenarian eyes," who will immortalize this blood in his work.

The image which dominates this poem is one which has a long history in Hernández. Javier Herrero is of the opinion that blood—a transcendental image which expresses in fine Hernández's world view—achieves the level of myth in Hernández's work. The word "blood" appears eight times and is the subject of every sentence but one in the sonnet.

In the first stanza blood represents the lives lost in the war: "It is two years of blood: it is two inundations." The use of the word "inundations" widens the meaning of blood: now it is associated with the primordial chaos, the Great Flood, the uroboric ocean. This association is reinforced in the next two verses: "Blood of solar action, you come ravening, / Until you leave the balconies deserted and drowned." The sun is usually a masculine image, but like the phallic images of the first period which represented the Great Mother's enslavement of the youth, the sun here represents a destructive side of masculinity which plays right into the hands of the devouring Earth Mother. Blood here represents a bestial bloodlust. The stanza expresses Hernández's dawning realization that war, rather than abetting liberation from the old bonds, can enslave one in a new bestiality, a new thralldom to the forces of the unconscious.

In the second stanza blood's now vanished traditional roles are mourned. The blood which used to represent the finer instinctual urges, especially sexual, belongs now to Hernández's and the world's past. Increasingly in the poems of *Man the Spy* Hernández sounds the cry that time is out of joint and that Nature has been turned upside down: "Look at it roiling seas, overtaking trains, / Discouraging bulls where it encouraged lions." The surrealistic quality of this image is eminently suited to describing the dislocations and irrationalities which the continuing war had caused. The lion, once a proud emblem of Hernández's comrades, seems to have disappeared with all of its passion. In its place are equally fierce but now disheartened bulls. They have been enervated by the very bloodlust which used to incite them.

It is in the third stanza that blood takes on an entirely new and wider significance. It is no longer just specific deaths, but mortality itself: time in our blood. In this wider sense the poet, although never wounded in the war, is like all of us (with our "bloods of every size"), "more than wounded," for we are all mortal, and the war's carnage reminds us forcibly of this mortality. Feeling "more than wounded" also suggests that the hurt goes beyond Hernández's flesh to his soul and beyond him, for mankind itself is being savaged in this war. In the fourth stanza blood is used once again to represent the fallen soldiers, still splendorous lights.

"July 18" lacks the careful organization of a sonnet like "Will it not cease . . . ," but compared to most of the war poetry it is highly structured. We do not find the classical sonnet sequence in which a dilemma or question is posed in the quatrains, with a resolution offered in the tercets. "July 18" is a lamentation: how could it have a resolution?

The first stanza introduces the motifs which will give the poem its coherence. (1) The floodlike quality of the blood which has been shed: "It is blood, not hail" (although it seems like hail, hard and damaging), "it is two inundations," so high they have flooded the balconies, so high they reach Hernández's temples. (2) The poet's intimate involvement in this cataclysm: the blood strikes his temples, causing him anguish (this is almost certainly a reference to

Hernández's debilitating headaches). (3) The close relationship between time and the war deaths. Time moves us inexorably toward our deaths in normal times: in war the rate accelerates. The "solar action" of the blood probably refers to the cyclical nature of the sun, which entails its death each night.

In the second stanza the time motif is seen in a change of verb tenses—"blood which is," "blood which used to"—as well as in the image of blood overtaking trains in disregard of timetables and established sequences. War upsets schedules, changes capriciously the amount of time each of us may be allotted. The flood motif reappears in the line: "Look at it roiling seas." Stanza 3 is primarily about the time / mortality aspect of the war and Hernández's intimate involvement with it: it circulates in his very veins. In Stanza 4 all three motifs are present. One cannot bathe death in this flood of blood, because the deaths are so many that even a deluge of blood would not suffice. The dead heroes with their bravery, and the poet with his work can defeat the war-accelerated threat of death (in a sense then, this poem has a resolution): both will live immortally.

In "July 18" we have a poem which suggests an abatement in zeal, a growing awareness that the cost of war is too great to be justified. Form and style are becoming important once again; the message has risen above the hortatory and the topical. With the exception of the two poems written to commemorate his trip to Russia, all of the poems in *Man the Spy* reflect to some extent this feeling of desolation, of infinite weariness. He writes about hunger, which is turning them into beasts; about the Nationalist prisons ("Las cárceles"), "factories of tears," "a well without exit"; about the wounded; and transport trains for the wounded:

> El tren lluvioso de la sangre suelta,
> el frágil tren de los que se desangran,
> el silencioso, el doloroso, el pálido,
> el tren callado de los sufrimientos.
>
> Van derramando piernas, brazos, ojos,
> van arrojando por el tren pedazos.
> Pasan dejando rastros de amargura,
> otra vía láctea de estelares miembros. (p. 335)
>
> The train slick with flowing blood,
> The fragile train of those who bleed,

> The silent, dolorous, pale,
> The hushed train of suffering.
>
> . . . .
>
> They go spilling legs, arms, eyes,
> They go throwing bits from the train.
> They pass by leaving a trail of bitterness,
> Another Milky Way of stellar limbs.

Even poems which attempt to strengthen his comrades' faltering resolve lack the earlier conviction that all will come out well, that death should not be feared. Before the clock and the dawn, Hernández was more than wounded.

The poetry and drama which Hernández produced during the war years is not a high point in his work if we judge it by aesthetic standards. But are we justified in judging it by such standards, or should we change the criteria by which we evaluate poetry written not to delight but almost exclusively to instruct? A considerable number of critics do believe that committed art should be judged differently. Space does not allow us to enter into the debate here,[14] nor would the reader's appreciation of Hernández's work be enhanced if we could. I think it unquestionable that the war poetry and drama were successful as social art; that given the horrific circumstances of that unequal struggle which he had to poeticize, Hernández wrote verse of remarkable quality. There are few who could read "The Train of the Wounded" or "Hunger" or "The Soldier and the Snow" without a catch in the throat, even if they had never heard of Miguel Hernández or Spain or the Civil War. Yet as a whole the work is too flawed to allow us to appreciate the sentiments; the diction, the mechanical repetitions, the slogans: all serve too often to distract—even repel—the reader.

The struggle to break away from the past and to formulate and establish a brave new world is an archetypal drive in man, such that the literature of this struggle is in some measure relevant to all of us. But Hernández himself realized before the war was in its last year that his vision of the new world had been faulty, that somewhere a more elemental truth awaited him. It is perhaps because his vision was flawed that much of the work of this period has not withstood the test of time and does not strike, as true art does, the chord of recognition and empathy in us all.

CHAPTER 4

The Last Years

I *Biographical Data*

AFTER his apprehension in Portugal, Miguel began what Ifach
has aptly named his "Calvary of incarceration" (p. 238). After
brutal interrogations, he was sent to Torrijos, a prison in Madrid.
From May until September he composed the majority of the poems
which make up the *Cancionero y romancero de ausencias (Songs
and Ballads of Absence)*. Various of his prison companions (among
them Antonio Buero Vallejo, who would emerge as Spain's leading
dramatist in the postwar period) recount Miguel's manner of composition, which depended on what he termed his best archive: his
memory. Miguel used to compose his poems in his head, reworking
and refining them until he was satisfied; only then did he commit
them to paper, which was too scarce to waste with first drafts.

In September, for reasons which are still disputed, Hernández
was released from prison.[1] He spent a few days in Madrid among his
friends, who advised him to flee the country immediately. He chose
to return to Orihuela and Josefina and Manolo, convinced (as Lorca
had been convinced when he returned to Granada) that nothing ill
could befall him among his own people. He brought with him a
notebook with the songs and ballads he had composed in prison,
where he had at last been forced to cease the frenetic pace he had
maintained during the war. There, too, the overwhelming personal
vicissitudes he had suffered all came into focus and resulted in the
book which is unquestionably the finest he ever wrote.

He was arrested and imprisoned once again before two weeks had
passed, betrayed by a jealous countryman. During the next year he
was transferred from prison to prison, sentenced to death, and then
granted a commutation to thirty years. He wrote very little poetry.
"You ask me if I have been writing anything but letters," he wrote to

126

a friend in June, 1941, almost two years after his first imprisonment, "and I must tell you no. It is impossible for me. And now, when I am going to be close to my family, even more impossible. Someday it shall come to pass" (cited in Guerrero Zamora, p. 167). He directed all of his energy and imagination to those letters, mostly to Josefina, but to other friends as well, urging their intercession, begging their help for Josefina and Manolillo. The correspondence to Josefina, only a few examples of which have been published (principally in Zardoya's and Ifach's biographies), presents a remarkable picture of Hernández. He was always attempting to raise her spirits, to infect her with his optimism, to convince her that he was not suffering as much as she imagined. They were often illustrated with little sketches to amuse Manolillo and Josefina's little sisters.

After more than a year of importuning the authorities, Miguel was transferred to a prison in Alicante, his twelfth and last place of detention. There he was able to see his family regularly. But this happiness was as short-lived as the others: within a few months he suffered an attack of bronchitis complicated with paratyphoid fever. Without medication, proper care, or nourishing food he was unable to fight the infection. It developed into pneumonia and progressed vertiginously.

During his three years of imprisonment Miguel had been visited by well-placed friends who entreated him to recant and to declare (even simulated) allegiance to Franco's government. With this they were certain they could secure his release. He refused, outraged that anyone could think he would betray himself or the cause to which he was so dedicated. "As if Miguel Hernández were some cut-rate whore!" he exploded to a friend (quoted in Couffon, p. 60). As he lay on his deathbed the authorities increased their pressure on him to recant, or at least to confess himself to a priest.[2] His only capitulation was for Josefina: he consented to having a priest marry them. Ifach suggests that he was concerned to establish Josefina as his "legal" wife in this society organized around the Catholic Church (p. 324).

He died early on the morning of March 28, 1942. It was the third anniversary of the war's end. His last words suggest that he no longer feared death for himself, but that he regretted the pain it would cause his beloved. "How unfortunate you are, Josefina!" ("¡Qué desgraciada eres, Josefina!") The "evil star" that had brought Miguel so many misfortunes in life had one more in store for him.

He who had written in "Neighbor of Death" that a cemetery whose
antiseptic niches were above ground was "the same as a village of
dried-out honeycombs" had continued:

> Yo no quiero agregar pechuga al polvo:
> me niego a su destino: ser echado a un rincón.
> Prefiero que me coman los lobos y los perros,
> . . . .
> Y es que el polvo no es tierra.
>
> La tierra es un amor dispuesto a ser un hoyo,
> dispuesto a ser un árbol, un volcán y una fuente.
>
> Mi cuerpo pide el hoyo que promete la tierra,
> el hoyo desde el cual daré mis privilegios de león y nitrato
> a todas las raíces que me tiendan sus trenzas.
> . . . .
> No quiero que me entierren donde me han de enterrar.
> Haré un hoyo en el campo y esperaré a que venga
> la muerte. . . . (pp. 243–44)

> I do not want to add my breast to this dust:
> I refuse its destiny: to be thrown into a corner.
> I prefer that the wolves and the dogs eat me.
> . . . .
> It's just that dust isn't earth.
> The earth is love, disposed to being a grave,
> Disposed to being a tree, a volcano and a fountain.
>
> My body needs the grave that the earth promises,
> The grave from which I will give my privileges of lion and nitrate
> To all the roots that tender me their braids.
> . . . .
> I do not want them to bury me where they would bury me.
> I will make a grave in the field and I will wait
> Until death comes. . . .

He had exclaimed:

> ¡Y qué buena es la tierra de mi huerto!:
> hace un olor a madre que enamora,,
> . . . .
> ¿Cuándo caeré, cuándo caeré al regazo
> íntimo y amoroso, donde halla
> tanta delicadeza la azucena?

> Debajo de mis pies siento un abrazo,
> que espera francamente que me vaya. . . . (p. 201)

> Oh, how good the earth of my garden!
> It exudes a fragrance like a mother's which enamors,
> . . . .
> When will I fall, when will I fall into the lap
> Intimate and loving, where the lily
> Finds such delicacy?

> Beneath my feet I feel an embrace
> Which is waiting openly for me. . . .

Yet he who had so loved the earth was to be buried in a niche: "All day, with Justino Marín, brother of Ramón Sijé, who accompanied me," Vicente Hernández told Claude Couffon, "we spent taking measures so that he would not be buried in the earth, like a pauper, but in a niche" (p. 26). And so he lies interred in Niche 1009 of the Cementerio de Nuestra Señora del Remedio, in Alicante.

II *The Last Works*

There are two groups of poems written during this period: *Cancionero y romancero de ausencias (The Songs and Ballads of Absence)*, ninety-eight poems written almost entirely during Miguel's first stay in prison in 1939; and twenty-five poems printed in the *Complete Works* under the title "Last Poems." The latter were written between 1938 (celebrating the birth of his first son) and 1941, when Hernández stopped writing altogether. Additional poems have been published in various other books and magazines subsequent to the appearance of the *Complete Works;* all but one are now available in the *Complete Poetic Works.*[3]

Consonant with the psychological changes which Hernández was undergoing, he now turned away from the large audiences he had hoped to reach during the war. "The lyric is the genre," Northrop Frye writes, "in which the poet . . . turns his back on his audience" (*Anatomy*, p. 171); it is the genre in which the poet speaks to himself, clarifying his inner vision and committing it to words. Hernández was learning that the "Treasure" was a liberation of the self from the world around it; a serene self-sufficiency achieved through understanding that death is not fearsome, but merely an extension of life. Intentionally, then, his audience had diminished from the great army of his comrades-in-arms, to his wife and child in the early period of his imprisonment (he wrote to Josefina: "My heart, more than a heart is a boarding house where the only boarders allowed are you with your child." [Letter dated March 25, 1940, cited in Guerrero Zamora, p. 158]), and finally to himself alone, as we see in the somber "Vuelo" ("Flight," pp. 423–24), "El hombre no reposa: quien reposa es su traje" ("Man Does Not Rest: Who Rests Is His Garment," p. 416), "Sigo en la sombra" ("I Continue in the Darkness," pp. 416–17), and "Eterna sombra" ("Eternal Shadow," pp. 431–32).

We shall first consider the formal aspects of the *Songs and Ballads of Absence*. Hernández prepared it as a book, so we may expect it to have some formal unity.[4] In the only monograph dedicated to this aspect of the *Songs*, Francisco Díez de Revenga concludes that Hernández achieved the most remarkable of fusions between form and content in this collection. "We consider . . . Miguel Hernández as a late link in the long chain of *poesía de tipo tradicional*, elaborated by educated authors through momentaneous, emotional expressive intuitions. . . . We are not speaking . . . of a simple reinterpretation of the popular tradition, but rather of Hernández, with his voice attuned to tradition, bringing to the tradition a series of original expressions which renew and enliven it, as in their time Lope de Vega and Gil Vicente did."[5]

The verse lengths in the collection are varied, ranging from two syllables to eleven, but the majority of the poems are *arte menor*, as the title suggests. Poems composed exclusively of hepta- or octosyllabic verses form a slight majority; the remainder of the compositions are truly examples of free verse, with unusual combinations of equally unusual verse lengths. This irregularity in verse gives the poems an authentically traditional touch, as Díez points out (p. 41), for "free verse" has a long history in Spanish popular poetry: the earliest anonymous lyrics are notoriously irregular. Occasionally Hernández reworked or incorporated parts of well-known traditional songs into the compositions of *Songs and Ballads of Absence*.[6]

The organization of most of the poetry is traditional, based on parallelisms and refrains. Yet only rarely does Hernández use pre–established strophic patterns; like Lorca, he preferred his own arrangements of lines. Díez identifies ten different forms of parallelism in the *Songs and Ballads*[7] in addition to the refrain, which he finds is used in its true sense in relatively few poems: numbers 21,

53, 62, and 67. Assonance is used occasionally but not to the extent we might expect in *poesía de tipo tradicional*. Frequently, the change of one word or one verb tense constitutes the only development from one stanza to the next:

> La cantidad de mundos
> que con los ojos abres,
> que cierras con los brazos.
>
> La cantidad de mundos
> que con los ojos cierras,
> que con los brazos abres. (p. 361)
>
> The quantity of worlds
> Which with your eyes you open,
> Which you close with your arms.
>
> The quantity of worlds
> Which with your eyes you close,
> Which with your arms you open.

The effect of repeating a stanza with only one change is to concentrate the reader's attention on the significance of that one change. Indeed, nearly all of the distinguishing structural characteristics of this poetry which we have already mentioned and one other, its brevity, are designed to focus our attention on one central image or thought. Brevity (for not only are the verses short but over half the poems have eight verses or less) is another mark of the traditional nature of this work. Its briefness and its traditionalism also result in its being enigmatic, amphibolic. Díez's comments about poem 11 could easily be applied to *Songs and Ballads* in general.

> Querer, querer, querer,
> ésa fué mi corona.
> Ésa es.
>
> Loving, loving, loving,
> That was my crown.
> And is.

Díez writes: "In the condensation and brevity of the thought lies perhaps the poem's greatest beauty, which translates itself into a

logical lack of thematic concreteness. The poem appears to have
been wrested from a larger context which leaves us in suspense and
perplexed" (pp. 42–43).

Another example of this intensification through condensation is
poem 21:

> En el fondo del hombre,
> agua removida.
>
> En el agua más clara,
> quiero ver la vida.
>
> En el fondo del hombre,
> agua removida.
>
> En el agua más clara,
> sombra sin salida.
>
> En el fondo del hombre,
> agua removida.
>
> In the depths of man,
> Roiled water.
>
> In the clearest water,
> I want to see life.
>
> In the depths of man,
> Roiled water.
>
> In the clearest water,
> A shadow dead-ended.
>
> In the depths of man,
> Roiled water.

Stanzas 1, 3, and 5 are the refrain, 2 and 4 the *mudanzas* or body of
the poem. Since the first lines of the *mundanzas* are the same, all of
the development in the poem depends on their second lines. In the
refrain Hernández describes the state of the world as he perceives
it: men filled with turbulent emotions, unsettled and alienated. In
the second stanza he expresses a wish that the turbulence around
him cease, so that he might see life once again in its natural, un-

roiled state. The chorus then reiterates the actual state of affairs. In the fourth stanza, Hernández tells us why he cannot have his wish: there is an evil deep within man, either inherent in him or forced upon him by circumstances and now irremediably trapped within. There is only one verb in the poem: "I want." The longing which is summed up in that word becomes the emotional focus of the poem. The unvarying refrain joins with the fourth stanza, so lifeless (lacking a verb and speaking of shadows), to show how impossible are the hopes expressed in "I want."[8] Ricardo Gullón believes that in all of Hernández's work "there is declared . . . that inexorable dialectic between hopeful nostalgia and the hopeless presentation of the world as it is";[9] certainly this poem exemplifies such a dialectic.

Antithesis is one of the most common of the stylistic devices found in *Songs and Ballads of Absence*. It is a common recourse in traditional verse, but I believe it appealed to Hernández for an even more important reason. It is a structural reflection of the dualism which so informed his thinking, first manifesting itself in religious or moral terms: winter is pure, summer sinful; purity is good, lust is evil; then in the facile dichotomizations of the war. In the last years of his life, Hernández perceived the very nature of life to be binary, although the opposites are sometimes reconciled—or complicated—by a third factor. This is not to say that Hernández saw life in terms of Hegel's dialectic. As Octavio Paz points out in his study of the poetic image in *El arco y la lira* (translated by Ruth L. C. Simms as *The Bow and the Lyre* [Austin: University of Texas Press, 1973]), in the Hegelian model thesis and antithesis never exist simultaneously: "The thesis is not produced at the same time as the antithesis; and both disappear to give place to a new affirmation that, in engulfing them, transmutes them" (p. 86). The poetic image or poem, on the other hand, "not only proclaims the dynamic and necessary coexistence of opposites, but also their ultimate identity" (p. 87).

A few of the dualities which Hernández ponders in this collection are: I-Thou, man-woman, love-hate, presence-absence, past-present, life-death, night-day, and happiness-sadness. The love poetry especially is binary, reflecting not only the sexual duality which Hernández had always seen as primary, but also the difference between physical and remembered love, past joys and present sorrows. "Besarse, mujer" ("To kiss each other, wife," no. 33), for example, is fully developed around the man-woman, sun-moon, life-death antitheses. Love is itself a conjunction of opposites, and as such it contains its own seed of destruction. At any moment it may be transformed into its opposite, hate or indifference, as we can see in the fragment cited immediately after "To kiss . . .":

Besarse, mujer,
al sol, es besarnos
en toda la vida.

Ascienden los labios
eléctricamente
vibrantes de rayos,
con todo el fulgor
de un sol entre cuatro.

Besarse a la luna,
mujer, es besarnos
en toda la muerte.

Descienden los labios
con toda la luna
pidiendo su ocaso,
gastada y helada
y en cuatro pedazos.
          . . .
To kiss each other, wife,
In the sun, is to kiss
In all of life.

The lips ascend
Electrically
Vibrant with rays,
With all the effulgence
Of one sun among four.

To kiss each other by the moon,
Wife, is to kiss
In all of death.

The lips descend
With all the moon
Seeking to set,
Spent and frozen
And in four pieces.

No pudimos ser. La tierra
no pudo tanto. No somos
cuanto se propuso el sol
en un anhelo remoto.
Un pie se acerca a lo claro,
en lo oscuro insiste el otro.
Porque el amor no es perpetuo
en nadie, ni en mí tampoco.
El odio aguarda un instante
dentro del carbón más hondo.
Rojo es el odio y nutrido.
El amor, pálido y solo.
Cansado de odiar, te amo.
Cansado de amar, te odio . . .
    ("[Después del amor]," p. 402)

. . .

We could not be. The earth
Could not do so much. We are not
As much as the sun proposed
In a long-ago yearning.
One foot approaches the clear,
The other insists upon darkness.
Because love is not eternal
In anyone, including me.
Hatred awaits its moment
Within the deepest coal.
Red is hatred and vigorous.
Love, solitary and pale.
Tired of hating, I love you.
Tired of loving, I hate you.
    ("[After Love]")

Illustrative of the pervasiveness of the binary principle, or of the "complementary contradictions," as Paz calls them (after Stéphane Lupasco), are the following pairs from *The Songs and Ballads of Absence*. (In every case the first line cited is the first line of the poem. The second either follows that line immediately or is the first verse of the second stanza.)

Si te perdiera . . .
Si te encontrara . . . (p. 367)

Cada vez más presente . . . .
Cada vez más ausente. . . . (p. 368)

Cogedme, cogedme.
Dejadme, dejadme. . . . (p. 369)

Tus ojos se me van
de mis ojos y vuelven . . .

Tu boca se me marcha
de mi boca y regresa . . .

Tus brazos se desploman
en mis brazos y ascienden . . . (p. 388)

Tan cercanos, y a veces
qué lejos nos sentimos,
tu yéndote a los muertos,
yo yéndome a los vivos. (p. 374)

Tú de blanco, yo de negro,
vestidos nos abrazamos.
Vestidos aunque desnudos
tú de negro, yo de blanco. (p. 371)

Tú eres fatal ante la muerte.
Yo soy fatal ante la vida. . . . (p. 377)

Hablo después de muerto.
Callas después de viva. . . . (p. 395)

If I were to lose you . . .
If I were to find you . . .

More and more present . . . .
More and more absent . . . .

Hold me, hold me.
Leave me, leave me . . . .

Your eyes slip away from me
And my eyes and return . . .

Your mouth leaves me
And my mouth and comes back . . .

Your arms collapse
In my arms and ascend . . .

So near, and at times
How far apart we feel ourselves.
You heading toward the dead,
I heading toward the living.

You in white, I in black,
Dressed we embrace each other.
Dressed although naked
You in black, I in white.

You are fatal in the presence of death.
I am fatal in the presence of life. . . .

I speak after dying.
You fall quiet after living. . . .

The trinary division appears with less frequency, but as Cano Ballesta notes, it "stands out in this book because of its novelty, relative insistence, and profound union with the themes" (p. 229). Some of the poems structured around the ternary are numbers 38 ("El corazón es agua," "The heart is water"), 42 ("¿Qué pasa?" "What's happening?"), 51 ("Son míos, ¡ay!, son míos," "They are mine, oh, they are mine"), 55 ("Rueda que irás muy lejos," "Wheel that will range so far"), 86 ("Uvas, granadas, dátiles," "Grapes, pomegranates, dates"), 90 ("Tristes guerras," "Sad wars"). The two most important poems in this class, however, are numbers 9 and 10, for they elucidate the three parts:

Llegó con tres heridas:
la del amor,
la de la muerte,
la de la vida.

Con tres heridas viene:
la del la vida,
la del amor,
la de la muerte.

Con tres heridas yo:
la de la vida,
la de la muerte,
la del amor.

He arrived with three wounds:
That of love,
That of death,
That of life.

With three wounds he comes:
That of life,
That of love,
That of death.

With three wounds I:
That of life,
That of death,
That of love.
Escribí en el arenal
los tres nombres de la vida:
vida, muerte, amor.

Una ráfaga de mar,
tantas claras veces ida,
vino y los borró.

　　. . .

I wrote on the sandy beach
The three names of life:
Life, death, love.

A blast of the sea,
So many times clearly gone,
Came and erased them.

Life and death can easily be pictured as antitheses, but how is love related to the two? In the first poem, he rearranges the "wounds" until their sequence seems to explain satisfactorily how he feels about them. Following basic principles of Spanish syntax, the last-mentioned element receives greatest emphasis. In the past, when he "arrived" or was born, he was the product of love, destined to death, but most "wounded" by the very necessity of living. The second stanza speaks of a possible future, when he will be alive and in love, but hounded by death. In the final stanza there is no verb: it is a timeless and static self Hernández describes to us: a being who is alive, and who thereby carries death's wound within, but whose most distinguishing and important characteristic is bearing love's wound. For love is a solution to the problem of death (which is also the problem of life). Love annihilates death in two ways, both of which Hernández considers at length in his poetry. First, it makes life momentarily so vivid, so splendid, that death is forgotten. Second, it assures man of perpetuation through his progeny.

> . . . ¡Qué absoluto portento!
> ¡Qué total fué la dicha de mirarse abrazados,
> . . . .
> . . . Fué tan cálidamente
> consumada la vida como el sol, su mirada.
> No es posible perdernos. Somos plena simiente.
> Y la muerte ha quedado, con los dos, fecundada. (p. 425)

> . . . What absolute portent!
> How complete the joy of seeing ourselves embracing,
> . . . .
> Life was as passionately
> . . . Consummated as the sun, its glance.
> It is not possible for us to be lost. We are pure seed.
> And death has been, with the two of us, fecundated.
>   . . .

> Para siempre fundidos en el hijo quedamos:
> fundidos como anhelan nuestras ansias voraces:
> en un ramo de tiempo, de sangre, los dos ramos,
> en un haz de caricias, de pelo, los dos haces.
> . . . .
> Con el amor a cuestas, dormidos y despiertos,
> seguiremos besándonos en el hijo profundo.
> Besándonos tú y yo se besan nuestros muertos,
> se besan los primeros pobladores del mundo. (pp. 412–13)

> Forever melded in the child shall we be:
> Melded as our voracious desires yearn:
> In one cluster of time, of blood, the two clusters,
> In one sheaf of caresses, of hair, the two sheaves.
> . . . .
> With love on our backs, asleep and awake,
> We will go on kissing in the depths of the child.
> When we are kissing each other our dead kiss,
> The first inhabitants of the world kiss.

It is principally in the poems dealing with the tangible result of their love, the child, that Hernández uses the ternary structure. It frequently appears in combination with the binary, because the couple is inextricably related to the child. The poem which begins "El sol, la rosa y el niño" (no. 76) is one of the poems most clearly organized around the binary-trinary structure. The first and third stanzas, which refer to the child, are tripartite; the second and fourth (their ordinal numbers are even, too) are bipartite. The second stanza is about the poet, who contrasts his present self (implicitly) with his future self. The fourth stanza presents another contrast: between the "tú" (you) who left and the poet who remains. This poem is one of the most amphibolic of the collection; in translation it is impossible to convey the variety of meanings which are left open in Spanish.

> El sol, la rosa y el niño
> flores de un día nacieron.
> Los de cada día son
> soles, flores, niños nuevos.
>
> Mañana no seré yo:
> otro será el verdadero.
> Yo no seré más allá
> de quien quiera su recuerdo.
>
> Flor de un día es lo más grande
> al pie de lo más pequeño.
> Flor de la luz el relámpago,
> y flor del instante el tiempo.
>
> Entre las flores te fuiste.
> Entre las flores me quedo. (p. 389)
>
> The sun, the rose, and the child
> Were born flowers of one day.
> Those of each day are
> New suns, flowers, children.
>
> Tomorrow I shall not be myself:
> Another will be the true one.
> I shall not be [exist] beyond
> He who might desire its [the day's] remembrance.
>
> The flower of one day is the greatest thing
> At the foot of the smallest.

> Flower of the light [is] the lightning flash,
> And flower of the instant is time.
>
> Among the flowers you left.
> Among the flowers I stay.

This poem touches upon the paradox of temporal existence. For a variety of reasons, Hernández has been called an Existential poet: in part because his poetry is always concerned with man as a physical being in a physical world, surrounded by others like himself; in part because of the fairly constant threat of death which he felt, and which colored his perceptions of life.[10] In this poem he considers another question which is frequently associated with Existentialist thinkers (although it did not originate with them): the insuperable difference, the "complementary contradiction" between objective and subjective time. Objectively, men live but a day in the life in the universe: they are "born flowers of one day." Manuel Ramón's life was exceptionally short, but from the universe's perspective ten months or thirty-two or seventy-four and a half years are not appreciably different. Human lives are instantaneous concretions of life, just as the lightning flash is an instantaneous manifestation of light. The subjective side of time is equally real. It is only through an individual human consciousness that the universe can be perceived. For all of its vastness, the universe might as well not exist if it could not register upon and elicit a response from the mind of man. Thus man, "the flower of one day is the greatest thing / At the foot of the smallest," which is the universe. Time in its infinity is merely the accretion of numberless personal instants: "And flower of the instant is time."

There is a further connection between man and time, for man is the being-in-time, the being who changes with time. When Hernández writes that the suns, roses, and children of each day are new, he speaks not only of new generations which replace the old, but also of the changes which occur in the same man from one day to the next. At each moment of his life, a man represents a new accumulation, has a new history (changed by the previous moment): is a new man. We see the influence of Antonio Machado and his Bergsonian conception of time in this idea. "Tomorrow I shall not be myself: / Another will be the true one." The old Miguel will only exist in memory. In the first line of this stanza there is also an echo of García Lorca's *Romance sonámbulo*. The father of the dead gypsy girl says to her dying lover: "Pero yo ya no soy yo, / ni mi casa es ya mi casa" ("But I am no longer myself, / Nor is my house any longer mine").[11] Like Miguel with his dead son, the girl's father was not himself because he was no longer a father.

The final couplet may be addressed to his wife or to his son. Like many of the poems in *Songs*, this couplet may be speaking to Josefina of the routes he and she followed in their grief over the child's death. On the other hand, the change in verb tenses (from the preterite, which describes the other's action and signifies that it was completed once and for all, and the present, which describes the poet's continuing state) would suggest the second possibility. It is the child who left abruptly, leaving his father among the new day's new flowers.

Even after as brief a consideration as ours it becomes evident that Hernández had indeed achieved a remarkable fusion between form—at every level—and content in the *Songs and Ballads of Absence*. The "Last Poems" of this period were composed before, contemporaneously, and after those of the *Songs and Ballads*.[12] They were never projected to form a book, so far as is known, and indeed, they lack the structural unity of the *Songs and Ballads*. The major poems in the collection are *arte mayor*, principally alexandrine. The *arte menor* included is similar to that of the *Songs and Ballads*: cryptic, impressionistic, sometimes surrealistic.[13] Organization into traditional stanzas is far more usual in the "Last Poems" than in the *Songs and Ballads*. All of the *arte mayor* poems take the form of quatrains or sonnets, whereas the poems of *arte menor* are evenly divided between those with fixed stanzas and those without. None of the various poetic forms which Hernández used in this period is new to his work. We find alexandrine quatrains, and *poesía de tipo tradicional*.

III   *Vocabulary*

In general the lexicon of this poetry is of the utmost simplicity and universality. There remain none of the vulgarity of the war work, none of the abstruseness of the first period. A few recondite or poetic words can be found, but they would seem to have been chosen for their musicality. There are several new trends in the diction of this period: a greatly increased use of celestial words, especially evident in the earliest of the "Last Poems," a new use of abstract substantives, particularly in *Songs and Ballads* and the late "Last Poems"; a preponderance of substantives and verbs over adjectives, which are almost nonexistent in the *Songs and Ballads*, and a correlatively canny use of verbs as the chief signifiers.

The celestial vocabulary is not new to Hernández; in addition to his lunar studies in *Expert in Moons*, Hernández used numerous sidereal words and references in the transitional, Neruda-influenced poems written before the war. But in the earliest of the "Last Poems" and in various poems of *Songs and Ballads* Hernández has turned all of his attention to the skies, wherein he finds metaphors for himself as father, for his parturient or nursing wife, and for his child. He would assimilate his life to the uranic rhythms, it appears, thereby identifying himself and his family as universal (or archetypal). "Through sex and the procreation of the child," Williams writes, "Miguel Hernández becomes one with the cosmos and the universe" (p. 170). He is the sun, his wife is the moon or night, his son the dawn, or new day. (We find no less than six different words for dawn.) Gabriel Berns suggests that these cosmogonic images grew out of Hernández's despair at the irredeemable condition of the world around him. "The physical world is almost completely transcended in these final poems. . . . In its place we find the explosion of a transparent light and the dawning of a new cosmos springing out of the destruction or at least the absence of a previously existent physical universe" (p. 145).

The increased use of abstract words reflects one of the salient characteristics of the poetry of this period (which in turn mirrors Hernández's psychological state), namely its retreat from the earthy sensuality of the first period and the hard corporeality of the second into a necessarily abstract world of memories and emotions. We find, for example, a whole series of words describing different states of sadness: *agonía, mal de las ausencias, desolacíon, ansia, angustia, lobregueces* (while it is impossible to reproduce the connotations of these words, especially as Hernández used them, they translate as: agony, the sickness of absence, desolation, yearning, anguish, gloominess). For absence or loneliness: *soledad, memoria, recuerdo, mal de las ausencias, agua de distancia, despedida, partir, partida, olvido* (solitude or loneliness, memory, remembrance, homesickness, water in the distance, farewell, leaving, departure, forgetfulness). Similar lists are easy to compile for loving, hatred, clarity, and obscurity. His attempt to define various feelings in terms of spatial concepts,[14] a technique which reminds us of Jorge Guillén, provides another series of abstract words: *ascensión, anchura, espesura, distancia, fondo, exaltactión, cumbre, decidido espacio* (ascension, width or extension, thickness, distance, depth, exaltation, peak, decided space). These abstract words, while seemingly precise, denote an intangible reality. The result is the same as in many of Guillén's "exact" compositions: extreme difficulty for the reader. Hernández complicates matters further, as Puccini observes, for "in order to represent his own condition of absence and anguish, constrained within a circumscribed course of certainties and doubts, the poet finds his most appropriate field of expression in the double or triple levels of meaning of the [objects or emotions] signified and of the signifiers [words], or else in circularity, in the interchangeableness and in the ambiguity of the linguistic signs" (p. 206). An example of this sort of amphibolic, although geometrically precise, poetry is the previously cited "To kiss each other, wife," or:

> El azahar de Murcia
> y la palmera de Elche
> para exaltar la vida
> sobre tu vida ascienden.

> El azahar de Murcia
> y la palmera de Elche
> para seguir la vida
> bajan sobre la muerte. (p. 387)

> The lemon blossom of Murcia
> And the date palm of Elche
> To exalt life
> Ascend over your life.

> The lemon blossom of Murcia
> And the date palm of Elche
> To follow life
> Descend over death.

The predominance of substantives and verbs over the less essential adjectives is logical given the briefness of the songs and ballads. A lack of modifiers serves to focus the reader's attention on the bare bones of the poem, thus intensifying its message. Diction here reinforces structure: both are designed to concentrate and intensify.

The verbs which are thrust into prominence by Hernández's constant paring take on exceptional force and expressiveness in this period. They become the organizational factors in the elliptical poems, key elements that the reader must decipher to understand the poetry.

> Negros ojos negros.
>
> El mundo se abría
> sobre tus pestañas
> de negras distancias.
>
> Dorada mirada.
>
> El mundo se cierra
> sobre tus pestañas
> lluviosas y negras. (pp. 361–62)
>
> Black eyes black.
>
> The world used to open
> Upon your eyelashes
> Of black distances.
>
> Golden gaze.
>
> The world closes
> Upon your eyelashes
> Rainy and black.

In this poem, for example, the change in verbs and in tense carries the whole message of the poem. The opening of a world is a happy, portentous event, yet because the verb "to open" is in the imperfect (past) tense, we know that it is no longer occurring.[15] Instead, the world closes now (and will probably continue to do so, as he suggests by using the simple present rather than the compound "is closing," which would have conveyed immediacy, not potential perpetuity). Two previously cited poems help to illustrate the pivotal nature of verbs. "In the depths of man" depends on the verb "I want" for coherence. In "He arrived with three wounds" the change in tenses from "arrived" to "comes," and the lack of any verb at all in the third stanza—where "am" is understood but not stated—also determines in great measure our interpretation of the life-death-love triptych.

"Sangre remota" ("Remote blood," no. 20) is a short description of the poet's frame of mind in the absence of his family. Since life

without them is unthinkable, Hernández uses no verb, allows no
life, in the poem:

> Sangre remota.
> Remoto cuerpo,
> dentro de todo.
>
> Dentro, muy dentro
> de mis pasiones,
> de mis deseos.
>
> Remote blood.
> Remote body,
> Within everything.
>
> Within, deep within
> My passions,
> My desires.

The hostile, deadened world of wartime is similarly described without verbs in "Entusiasmo del odio" ("Enthusiasm of hatred,"
no. 43), "Bocas de ira" ("Mouths of ire," no. 46), and "(Guerra)"
("[War]," no. 93), which I quote:

> La vejez de los pueblos.
> El corazón sin dueño.
> El amor sin objeto.
> La hierba, el polvo, el cuervo.
> ¿Y la juventud?
>
> En el ataúd.
>
> El árbol solo y seco.
> La mujer como un leño
> de viudez sobre el lecho.
> El odio sin remedio.
> ¿Y la juventud?
>
> En el ataúd.
>
> The old age of the villages.
> The heart without owner.

Love without an object.
Grass, dust, crow.
And the youth?

In the grave.

The tree solitary and dried out.
The woman like a log
Of widowhood on the bed.
Hate without remedy.
And the youth?

In the grave.

Pablo Luis Ávila underlines the importance of verbs in all phases of Hernández's work: "It is perhaps the verbs which are of the greatest interest for an analytical study of Hernández's poetry. By this means the poet is able to detach himself from the real element ([represented by] substantives either inanimate or of immutable essence) to enter, or more exactly to ascend to a stage where space, to all effects outside of time, acquires a decisive importance. Space understood as such and as a channel of regression, of flight, of negation of the ambient reality" (p. 156). Verbs, then, become another element within which Hernández increases the abstract quality of this work. Ávila's analysis of the previously cited "To kiss each other, wife" (see p. 134) shows how Hernández is able to use an action verb abstractly. "The lips ascent / Electrically": "This ascension dictated by longing, by absence and passion, is nothing other than the displacement of a kiss from the real plane where love is unrealizable to an unreal plane where the kiss is consummated symbolically" (p. 156).

IV *Stylistic Aspects*

While Hernández continued to use the longer verse he had adopted for the war poetry in most of the "Last Poems," the conversational syntax, rapid changes of subject, and frequent direct address have disappeared. There is little hyperbaton or syntactical ellipsis in these poems, but the frequent use of parallelism, correlation, plurimembration, and accumulation (see p. 29), above) marks the diction of these works as unmistakably poetic. A few examples of correlation (the second example is a freer correlation than we might have found in the first period):

La vida (A_1), la luz (A_2) se ahonda
entre muertos (B_1) y barrancos (B_2). (p. 421)

Life, light sinks down
Among the dead and the canyons.

. . .

Cásida[16] del sediento

Arena del desierto (A_1)
soy: desierto de sed (B_1).
Oasis es tu boca (C_1)
donde no he de beber (D_1).

Boca, oasis abierto (C_2)
a todas las arenas del desierto (A_2).

Húmedo punto en medio (C_3)
de un mundo abrasàdor, (E_1)
el de tu cuerpo, el tuyo (C_4)
que nunca es de los dos (D_2).

Cuerpo: pozo cerrado (C_5, D_3)
a quien la sed (B_2) y el sol (E_2)
han calcinado. (p. 417)

Plaint of the Thirsting Man

Sand of the desert
Am I: a desert of thirst.
Your mouth is an oasis
Where I am not to drink.

Mouth, oasis open
To all the sands of the desert.

A humid speck in the midst
Of a burning world,
That of your body, yours
And never ours.

Body: a sealed well
Whom thirst and the sun
Have calcined.

In the *Songs and Ballads of Absence* the syntax is connotative rather than denotative. Incomplete sentences are the norm and ellipsis, in syntax and in significance, is common. Parallelistic sentence structuring, already considered under *Structure*, is so common that "in fact, it characterizes this book," in Cano Ballesta's words (p. 249).

In the last poetry we find apostrophe (to his absent wife and sons, and later to himself), anaphora, oxymorons, paradox and, especially, metaphors. Anaphora is a device common to traditional, parallelistic verse. Like all the other forms of repetition, it serves to intensify. Oxymorons and paradox reflect not only the antithetical style and message of much of this poetry, but also several of its themes: the melding of the opposites in the hierogamy or *hieros gamos* (Greek for "sacred marriage," this term is used to describe pairs whose conjunction is eminently fruitful and creative), the dichotomy between reality and aspiration. The poem "Sonreír con la alegre tristeza del olivo" ("To Smile With the Joyous Sadness of the Olive Tree," p. 422) has a number of oxymorons and paradoxes: "esta alegre y triste vanidad" ("this happy and sad vanity"), "esta sonrisa tan clara y tan sombr´ıa" ("this smile so bright and so shadowy"). Others include "Triste instrumento alegre de vestir" ("Sad instrument for dressing and happy," p. 424), "Cada ciudad, dormida, despierta . . . / de sueño que arde y llueve" ("Each city, asleep, awake . . . / Of a dream which burns and rains," p. 424), "Piedras de plumas, muros de pájaros" ("Stones of feathers, walls of birds," p. 427), "muda, pero sonora" ("mute, but sonorous," p. 430), "brillantemente sombrío" ("Brilliantly shadowy," p. 380), "El mar gime sed ("The sea moans of thirst," p. 397).

Metaphor, both epiphoric and diaphoric, is a key element in the last poetry. Díez has spoken of the unexpected and brilliant contrasts which give this poetry much of its force: "often it will be the contrast, painful, surprising and pathetic, which will replace a whole set of repetitive recourses in search of the exact and true expression" (p. 40). This startling note of contrast is frequently achieved by a simple diaphoric linking of images:

> Troncos de soledad,
> barrancos de tristeza
> donde rompo a llorar. (p. 383)

Trunks of solitude,
Ravines of sadness
Where I burst into tears.

. . .

Niño: ala, rueda, torre.
Pie. Pluma. Espuma. Rayo.
Ser como nunca ser. (p. 380)

Child: wing, wheel, tower.
Foot. Feather. Froth. Lightning.
Being as it has never been.

Most of the poems have a combination of epiphor and diaphor, as in "Grapes, pomegranates, dates" (no. 86), "(War)," (pp. 397–98), and "Body of a Clarity Which Nothing Dims" (pp. 426–27). In many cases the difficulty of this verse derives from Hernández's use of metaphors, for often the vehicle has neither a universal tenor nor any precedent in his work:

Llevadme al cementerio
de los zapatos viejos.

Echadme a todas horas
La pluma de la escoba.

Sembradme con estatuas
de rígida mirada.

Por un huerto de bocas
futuras y doradas
relumbrará mi sombra. (p. 401)

Carry me to the cemetery
For old shoes.

Throw me at all hours
The pen of the broom.

Sow me with statues
Fixedly staring.

All through an orchard of mouths,
Future and golden,
My shadow will shine forth.

The peculiar juxtaposition of cemeteries for old shoes, the pen of a broom, and rigidly staring statues perplexes the reader at first. It is only after considerable discursion that we arrive at the probable meaning of the poem. Old shoes are commonly used as emblems of once useful, now forgotten objects. Conceivably the imprisoned Hernández felt similarly useless and forgotten. The pen of the broom is a more perplexing image, but it can be clarified if we look at a sonnet from "Last Poems" written in the Torrijos prison in September, 1939—i.e., when Hernández was also working on the *Songs and Ballads*. (Frequently the "Last Poems," with their longer lines and far less elliptical style, help to illuminate the cryptic *Songs and Ballads*.) The sonnet, "Ascensión de la escoba" ("Ascension of the Broom," pp. 429–30) describes the apotheosis of the lowly broom—it is in fact a Christ figure which "Para librar del polvo sin vuelo cada cosa / bajó, porque era palma y azul, desde la altura" ("In order to free all things from flightless dust / It descended, for it was a palm and blue, from the heights")—into a mystical tongue "sublime y acordada" ("sublime and harmonious"). The broom is thus praised because it is associated with work, the poor man's source of pride. When Hernández here demands that he be thrown the pen of the broom, he is speaking of the new sort of work he has had to do in prison. His old implement of work, the pen, has been replaced by a broom. He accepts this, commands it: let his labor be his poem.

The statues fixedly staring refer to funerary statuary in the sort of cemetery where Hernández did not wish to be buried. These three couplets, then, tell of Hernández's new existence, one mandated by captors and designed to humiliate or break its victims. Yet he turns the tables on these men who control his body, for they can never control his mind. He does not passively accept what they have done to him, for at least within the confines of this poem he is in command and gives *them* orders: Do with me what you will, for *I* will it. Moreover, after you have finished—and are moldering in your graves—my shadow will shine forth in the mouths of future generations.

In another deceptively simple poem, "Hold me, hold me" (no. 25) we can further appreciate Hernández's thoroughly personal use of metaphor.

> Cogedme, cogedme.
> Dejadme, dejadme.

Fieras, hombres, sombras.
Soles, flores, mares.

Cogedme.

Dejadme.

Hold me, hold me.
Leave me, leave me.

Wild animals, men, shadows.
Suns, flowers, seas.

Hold me.

Leave me.

What sort of contrast is being made between the third and fourth verses? Or are all six substantives coexistent in the world, or in the poet? We can only make an educated guess, based on Hernández's previous use of these symbols. In the third period wild animals and shadows consistently refer to man's base and feral instincts, which Hernández had come to believe ineradicable. Men are trapped, literally and figuratively, between the two. Suns and flowers are ephemera (cf. "The sun, the rose and the child"), and so is the sea in its trackless, ever-changing immensity.

The six substantives, then, would seem to describe two aspects of man: his inherent evil, and his mortality (both of which resulted from that first Fall. As Puccini has so astutely observed, Hernández "always proceeds within a lexicon, a symbology, a stylistic and linguistic texture of clear Renaissance and Baroque descent, with all of its recourses of Biblical and Christian mythology" [p. 150]. For all of his rejection of the Church, his thinking had been molded by her priests, from Calderón to his Orihuelan mentor, Don Luis Almarcha.) How are the imperatives, "hold me" and "leave me," related to these facets of man? Hernández addresses the commands to a plural you, so we must suppose he is speaking to the beasts, men, shadows, to the suns, flowers and seas. When one aspect of man seems to overwhelm him, e.g., his bestiality, does Hernández then call out for death (or mortality) to take him? When he finds himself close to death, does he implore even his bestial side to save him from death's nothingness? Does he simply wish to renounce his humanity altogether, since "Leave me" is his final command? Another brief poem would appear to support the latter interpretation:

> Me tendí en la arena
> para que el mar me enterrara,
> me dejara, me cogiera.
> ¡ay de la ausencia! (p. 433)

> I stretched out on the sand
> So the sea would inter me,
> Would leave me, would seize me.
> Oh, absence!

V *Themes*

The themes of this period center around Hernández's discovery and exaltation of the inner values as the only truth in life. The egocentric fears and desires of the first period are gone, as are the bellicosity and political aims of the second. Once again, we divide these themes somewhat arbitrarily for the purpose of discussion.

1. The I-Thou relationship. It is as part of a couple, Hernández realizes, that man is able to develop his full potential, both personally and in relation to others in the world. The archetypal term for this creative and fruitful union is *hieros gamos*. The couple is also the means for each member's perpetuation through its offspring. The pregnant wife, "madre iluminada" ("luminous mother"), grows out of this theme and the next. Gabriel Berns believes that Hernández sought to construct a whole new world within the confines of this relationship. Commenting on "El número de sangres" ("The number of bloods," pp. 365–66), he writes: "It is suggested that all creation has come to reside within this 'tú y yo' [Thou and I] and all that existed outside the speaker and the loved one is now to remain below the surface . . ." (p. 129). It is only within this microcosm, according to Berns, that Hernández perceives "light and the possibility of perpetuation since its primarily hermetic nature will seal it off from time and other destructive elements. As a consequence of this new vision, the earth as a source of the life force has been replaced by the figure of the woman in whose womb the poet now

sees concentrated all the sought-after clarity and the permanence which are to prevail in this inner world" (p. 140).

2. The establishment of the family. The love which Hernández felt for his two sons and his aspirations to perpetuation through them reverberate through this poetry. His wife's pregnancies are sung in cosmic terms: he and she are sky and earth, the *hieros gamos;* the child is "the son of the light and of the shadow."

3. Frustration of the union, by absence, by war, by grief. In the last poems every theme seems to have a counter-theme, every emotion a counter-emotion, attesting on a thematic level to what we have already pointed out at the stylistic level: Hernández's belief that the world is antithetical, filled with "complementary contradictions." In theme 1 the *hieros gamos* is sung in its fulfillment; here its defeat by hostile forces is lamented. The son who was briefly a part of the family unit inspired "a joy forever unique" and then the blackest despair. Hernández summarized life's contradictions in a *copla de soledad* (three octosyllabic verses, the first and third assonant) which appears in Losada's *Antología* (p. 169):

No vale entristecerse,
la sombra que te lo ha dado,
la sombra que se lo lleve.

It is not worth grieving,
The shadow which has given you it,
May the shadow take it away.

4. The exaltation of inner values: brotherhood, love, freedom, peace, truth. The three previous themes also praise such values as they relate to his own family. The poems which we include under theme 4, however, are of a more general philosophical nature, directed to all men. They include some of the poems in *Songs and Ballads*, and many of the latest poems in "Last Poems."

5. Centroversion. This is a psychological term used by Jung to denote a final consolidation of the ego and a stabilization of consciousness in the face of death. It is in the very last poems which Hernández wrote that we find this theme. Drawing away from his earthly attachments—we find only an occasional mention of his family in the last poems—Hernández sought the understanding and inner peace that could reconcile him to his death.

The archetypal patterns underlying Hernández's poetry are as evident in this period as in the earlier ones. The Transformation Myth (or the Captive and the Treasure, which we explained briefly in the previous chapter; see Chapter 3, note 11) is now the dominant archetype. When the Hero has killed the World Parents, he releases the Captive, who is a personal, not archetypal, woman with whom he can enter into a fruitful union. They establish a permanent relationship and begin their family. It is evident in Hernández's poetry that Josefina is as important to him in her role as mother of his child as she is in her role as wife. "No te quiero a ti sola: te quiero en tu ascendencia / y en cuanto de tu vientre descenderá mañana" ("I do not love you alone: I love you for your ancestry / And for what will descend from your womb tomorrow," p. 412).

Once the Hero has reached this stage of wholeness he can move on to discover the nature of the Treasure, "the precious thing hard to obtain." The Treasure is not tangible like the Captive. It is an understanding of the nature of life and death, or as Campbell says, of "the true relationship of the passing phenomena of time to the imperishable life that lives and dies in all" (p. 328). The Hero's reaction to the realization of death may be extroverted, in which case he goes out and seeks to change the world; or introverted, as was Hernández's. The introvert searches within himself and discovers those inner values of which we have spoken, "exalting them as knowledge and wisdom, as a law and a faith, a work to be accomplished and an example to be followed" (Neumann, *Origins*, p. 220).

Finally the psyche enters the stage of consolidation (or centroversion) in which it draws away from its outside detachments in order to reflect upon itself. The ideal result of this reflection is a synthesis between ego and self, or the conscious and the unconscious. Once again in the ego's history there appears a symbol representing a synthesis of opposites: called the uroboros in the emergent phases, it is now called the mandala. "To the maturing psyche, slowly integrating itself under the sign of the hermaphrodite, the world, too, assumes the appearance of the hermaphroditic ring of existence. . . . Humanity as a whole and the single individual have the same task, namely, to realize themselves as a unity" (Neumann, *Origins*, p. 417).

It has become evident in both our structural and thematic studies of the poetry of the last period that Hernández had become acutely aware of the hermaphroditic nature of the world. Yet we can only conjecture about his reaching that final stage—the synthesis of his own psyche, with its concomitant vision of the world's unity—for he wrote no poetry in the last nine months of his life. The result of true centroversion, psychologically speaking, is the conquest of death, for death is the primordial symbol for the decay and dissolution of the personality. If Hernández felt that death—fear of which had inspired so much of his poetry—was no longer a threat in those last months, if he was finally at peace with himself and his destiny, then perhaps he felt no further need to create. Thus might his final silence (for he was not sick during all of those months) be explained. In one of the last letters he is known to have written, dated January 26, 1942, Hernández consoles his friend Carlos Rodríguez Spiteri on the death of his father. The words, paradoxical and detached, suggest Hernández was preparing himself philosophically for death: ". . . The very rapid progression of the disease and its end must have surprised and wounded you doubly. That is how it has happened to me. Everything passes away and everything lingers on. . . . Be consoled in every way, and the most important thing, for nothing is important, is to give a beautiful solution to life" (cited in Guerrero Zamora, p. 169 n.).

The four universal themes which we have followed through Hernández's earlier periods remain important in the last work. Sex is glorified in the poems written around the birth of the first son, especially in the tripartite "Son of the Light and of the Shadow," both because of the joy and communion it brings the couple, and for its fruit, the child. This is essentially unchanged from the second period except that the power of the sexual act to meld physically the already spiritually united *hieros gamos* is now emphasized.

Love is the quintessential theme of this period. In the early poems it is a physical and spiritual love for his wife, pregnant with his child; then for his first son. In the *Songs and Ballads of Absence* this familiar love undergoes a transmutation corresponding to Hernández's imprisonment and separation from his loved ones: love becomes a remembered, an almost abstract, emotion. Hernández's love for his second son partakes of this abstraction, for he knows the child almost solely through pictures and Josefina's letters. In the first long hours of solitude and repose which Hernández has been able to enjoy in more than three years of war, he begins to muse about brotherhood and war and the nature of man. He reviles war because he believes it thwarts love, just as absence does. But as his vision grows more somber, he begins to doubt that other men have any natural love to be thwarted: perhaps war is the natural state, love the unnatural. In the last few poems love means charity in the Christian sense, a state of being so committed to love that all the world is a Thou.

Several of Hernández's critics have discussed the role of love in these last works, none more provocatively than Marie Chevallier, who believes that Hernández early in his life invented a "religion of love" when he found the Christian religion lacking. When he pondered the war from his prison perspective, he concluded that "the lack of love is the evil, the misfortune, the death, the destiny, and constitutes a central emptiness in the order of the world and of man." To counter the lack of love which he perceives around him, Chevallier writes, Hernández proposes a "freedom to love" (*libertad de amor*), for the gift of love, freely given in response to hatred, proves and establishes man's liberty. She then cites part of poem 97, "(Después del amor)" ("[After Love]"):

> Amor: aleja mi ser
> de sus primeros escombros,
> y edificándome, dicta
> una verdad como un soplo.

> Love: distance my being
> From its first ruins,
> And in constructing me, dictate
> A truth like a gust of wind.

"Here begins man's dominion over his destiny. It is the lesson which Miguel Hernández learns from the experience of the war. For hatred he substitutes the call of love. That is the last word taken from what he knows about himself, man creates man" (p. 25).[17]

The thought of death was never far from Miguel's mind. Added to the carnage of the war in which so many of his friends had perished, the loss of Manuel Ramón brought death especially close to him. He saw his own death in the child's, and thus his mourning was both for the child and for himself. This is nowhere so explicit as in the poem "The Child of the Night" (pp. 425–26), where his alternation of first and third person verbs erases the normal semantic distinctions between what is I and not-I: he and his child are the same.

Riéndose, burlándose con claridad del día,
se hundió en la noche el niño que quise ser dos veces.
No quiso más la luz. ¿Para qué? No saldría
más de aquellos silencios, de aquellas lobregueces.

Quise ser . . . ¿Para qué? . . . Quise llegar gozoso
al centro de la esfera de todo lo que existe.
Quise llevar la risa como lo más hermoso.
He muerto sonriendo serenamente triste.

Niño dos veces niño: tres veces venidero.
Vuelve a rodar por ese mundo opaco del vientre.
Atrás, amor. Atrás, niño, porque no quiero
salir donde la luz su gran tristeza encuentre.

Regreso al tigre plástico que alentó mi inconsciencia.
Vuelvo a rodar, consciente del sueño que me cubre. (p. 425)

Laughing, joking with the brightness of the day,
There collapsed into the night the child I twice tried to be.
He no longer wanted the light. For what? He would not emerge
Again from those silences, from that gloom.

I tried to be . . . For what? . . . I tried joyfully to reach
The center of the sphere of all that exists.
I tried to bear the smile as the greatest beauty.
I have died smiling serenely sad.

Child twice a child: three times coming.
Go back to circling within that opaque world of the womb.
Back, love. Back, child, for I do not want
To emerge where the light may find its great sadness.

I return to the plastic tiger which inspired my unconscious.
I circle again, aware of the sleep which covers me.

As he grew more contemplative, Hernández spoke less explicitly of
death and more of the need for love. With the exception of "The
Fields Hushed . . .," none of the last poems mentions death, although it hovers about in the background, as we shall see in "I
Continue in the Darkness."

The poet's quest for eternal return is more intense in the early
part of this period than ever before. He suggests in "Carry me to the

cemetery" that his name will live on because of his poetry, but his principle hope for transcendence lies with his son. Both the *Songs and Ballads* and the early poems of "Last Poems" are filled with this hope. As we have seen in "The Child of the Night," Hernández identifies his son as a reincarnation of himself. In poem 51 he writes that he is linked to all men, past, present and future, through the child:

> Son míos, ¡ay!, son míos
> los bellos cuerpos muertos,
> los bellos cuerpos vivos,
> los cuerpos venideros.
> Son míos, ¡ay!, son míos
> a través de tu cuerpo.

> They are mine, oh, they are mine,
> The beautiful dead bodies,
> The beautiful living bodies,
> The bodies to come.
> They are mine, oh, they are mine
> Through your body.

The infant's death suddenly blasted all of these illusions. Nor could Hernández any longer believe in that organic, agricultural rebirth which he had described (and relied upon) in his earlier periods. As Gabriel Berns writes of the last poems "this cycle [of life-death-rebirth] is incomplete, permanently out of phase. . . . The earth, which had been both the repository of the dead and the source of new life, has lost its dual character to become primarily a terminal thing, an end without a new beginning" (p. 134).

> Llueve sobre tus dos ojos
> negros, negros, negros, negros,
> y llueve como si el agua
> verdes quisiera volverlos.

> ¿Volverán a florecer?

> Si a través de tantos cuerpos
> que ya combaten la flor
> renovaran su ascua . . . Pero
> seguirán bajo la lluvia
> para siempre, mustios, secos. (pp. 393–94)

It rains on your two eyes
Black, black, black, black,
And it rains as if the water
Would like to turn them green.

Will they flower again?

If through so many bodies
Which presently combat the flower
They were to rekindle their glow . . . But
They will continue beneath the rain
Forever, withered, dry.

VI   *Symbols and Motifs*

There are few new symbols in the last period; in general Hernández used symbols whose general significance he had already established. The *hieros gamos* for example is often signified with the love/lust symbols of the first period: door, fire, pomegranate, blood, water, eyes, smells, feet and walking, the sexual act as death, and shadow. Yet there is a difference between the symbology of the first period and the last, in spite of the use of the same vehicles. The abstract ideas with which Hernández struggled in the last years could only be conveyed in polysemous symbols. For example, Hernández uses shadow or darkness ("sombra") throughout the three periods to denote the feminine. In the last period it signifies not only woman—see "(El último rincón)" ("[The Last corner]," pp. 399–400) and the first part of "Son of the Light and of the Shadow"—but also spiritual darkness, a being swallowed up by adverse circumstances, as in "Eternal Shadow" and "I Continue in the Darkness."

Similarly, water becomes polyvalent in the third period, whereas it had previously been a rather straightforward representation of the woman. In a few of the war poems, clear, pure water—explicitly or implicitly contrasted to stagnant or muddy water—symbolized the Republicans. In the earliest of the last poems, water continues to represent woman (see "Shores of Your Womb"). When he is away from her and her body is only a memory, her "water" becomes a mirage: "Your mouth is an oasis / Where I am not to drink."

Un agua de distancia
quiero beber: gozar
un fondo de fantasma. (p. 372)

> A distant water
> I wish to drink: to savor
> A phantom reservoir.

Water is also used to refer to man's spiritual status as in "In the depths of man," in which roiled water signifies man's bestial urges, or in poems 32, 43, and 97. Finally, Hernández uses water in its most elementary archetypal sense, as the container of opposites. In the *Songs and Ballads* it is one more way of representing the antithetical nature of life (see poems 8, 38, 75, and 80). In "The Fields Hushed," the rain joins together the dead and the living, erasing the distinctions between them. It is, then, mandalic.

There are two important new motifs which Hernández introduced in writing about the couple: the house (see below, p. 169) and the refulgent mother, around which he wrote several poems: "I Want No Other Light Than That of Your Body Before Mine," "Desde que el alba quiso ser alba" ("Ever Since the Dawn Wanted to Be Dawn," p. 420), and "Body of a Clarity Which Nothing Dims." In these poems the wife glows from the light of the sun she carries within her or from the milk with which she overflows.

For his sons, Hernández used many of his traditional masculine symbols. See for example the poem cited above, p. 78. The fig tree, feet and walking, rivers, light, sun, motion, towers, and others appear. Since Manuel Ramón died so young, Hernández referred to him with at least two of the symbols for transitoriness that he had applied to himself in the first period: flowers and the seasons. New symbols for this include migrating birds and the suns of each day. The child died in October, a month when birds fly south to escape the cold of winter, and a month when the sun's life grows briefer each day. (See especially "A mi hijo" ["To My Son"], pp. 414–15.)

In poems dealing with the failure or frustration of the conjugal pair, Hernández uses many symbols, familiar from early poems, for the Terrible Mother or the self-destructive male principle: noise, wind, hurricanes, rocks, dust, axes, the moon, beasts, teeth and biting, darkness or shadow and night. These represent all the forces, external or internal, which seek to separate and destroy the couple. Note the use of the house as refuge and symbol of their conjugal state:

> ¿Qué quiere el viento de enero
> que baja por el barranco
> y violenta las ventanas
> mientras te visto de abrazos?

Derribarnos. Arrastrarnos.

Derribadas, arrastradas,
las dos sangres se alejaron.
¿Qué sigue queriendo el viento
cada vez más enconado?

Separarnos. (p. 390)

What does the January wind want
That it comes down the ravine

And breaks in through the windows
While I dress you in my arms?

To fell us. To drag us down.

Felled, dragged down,
The two bloods receded.
What else does the wind want
More bitter by the moment?

To separate us.

To represent those new values which he gleaned from his intro-
spection, Hernández used—once again—symbols that had appeared
in earlier work. Water and shadow, discussed above, are two of
these symbols, and their polyvalency is typical of this group. Others
are foam, birds, hearts, rose, tomb, light, arms or embracing, the
mandala, and the motif of freedom. The heart or the womb of his
beloved becomes a new universe, within whose confines he can build
his ideal world (Berns, Chap. IV). The womb and the tomb, commonly assimilated in primitive thought, merge in this poetry: the
womb is "the last corner":

El último y el primero:
rincón para el sol más grande,
sepultura de esta vida. . . .
. . . .
Ay, el rincón de tu vientre;
. . . .
Allí quisiera tenderme
para desenamorarme.
Después del amor, la tierra.
Después de la tierra, nadie. (pp. 399–400)

The last and the first:
Corner for the greatest sun,
Sepulture of this life. . . .
. . . .

> Oh, the corner of your womb;
> . . . .
> There would I wish to stretch out
> To grow indifferent.
> After love, the earth.
> After the earth, no one.

The mandala, or symbol representing the integration of antitheses, does not have an archetypal form, for it is a symbol unique to each artist. "This is the hero's ultimate difficult task. How render back into light-world language the speech-defying pronouncements of the dark? . . . How translate into terms of 'yes' and 'no' revelations that shatter into meaninglessness every attempt to define the pairs of opposites?" (Campbell, p. 218). Hernández used no single symbol but rather a number of them, as well as a series of paradoxes and oxymorons, to try to render the vision he was groping toward. Let us briefly begin our analyses of representative poems with "I Continue in the Darkness," one of the last two or three poems he wrote. It shows Hernández struggling for such a synthetic vision.

VII   *Analysis of Poems*

> Sigo en la sombra, lleno de luz; ¿existe el día?
> ¿Esto es mi tumba o es mi bóveda materna?
> Pasa el latido contra mi piel como una fría
> losa que germina caliente, roja, tierna.
>
> Es posible que no haya nacido todavía,
> o que haya muerto siempre. La sombra me gobierna.
> Si esto es vivir, morir no sé yo qué sería,
> ni sé lo que persigo con ansia tan eterna.
>
> Encadenado a un traje, parece que persigo
> desnudarme, librarme de aquello que no puede
> ser yo y hace turbia y ausente la mirada.
>
> Pero la tela negra, distante, va conmigo
> sombra con sombra, contra la sombra hasta que ruede
> a la desnuda vida creciente de la nada. (pp. 416–17)[18]

> I continue in the *darkness*, full of *light;* does day exist?
> Is this my *tomb* or my *maternal vault?*
> The throb passes against my skin like a *cold*

Gravestone which germinates *warmly*, red, *tender*.

It is possible that I have *not yet* been *born*,
Or that I *have always died*.
If this is *living*, I do not know what *dying* might be,
Nor do I know what it is I pursue with such eternal yearning.

Chained to a garment, it seems that I pursue
Denuding myself, freeing myself from that which cannot
Be me and which makes the gaze turbulent and distant.

But the black cloth, *distant, accompanies* me
Shadow to shadow, against the shadow until it rolls on
To the naked *burgeoning life* of *nothingness*. (Italics mine.)

This alexandrine sonnet exemplifies the questing, philosophical tone of Hernández's last work. He explicitly speaks of denuding himself, or drawing away from the life he has known, to turn inward. Thus there is no mention of family, or absence. We are in a disembodied world, with "yearnings," "nothingness," something "which cannot be" the poet. Even light and darkness have lost all but a tinge of their physical connotations and refer instead to states of mind, as they do in the magnificent "Eternal Shadow":

Fuera, la luz en la luz sepultada.
Siento que sólo la sombra me alumbra.
Sólo la sombra. Sin astro. Sin cielo. (p. 431)

Outside, the light interred in light.
I feel that only the shadow illuminates me.
Only the shadow. Without a star. Without a sky.

He does not know what he will find within: all is new, uncharted. His perplexity is reflected syntactically in the questions of the first quatrain and in the tentative quality of the subjunctives of the second, as well as in the repetition of "I do not know."

The most prominent figures of speech in this sonnet are paradox and oxymoron, which I have italicized in the translation. Hernández was searching for a revelation, for a vision in which the seemingly irreconcilable opposition between life and death, hatred and love (shadow and light) might be resolved. The poem suggests that in spite of the apparent proximity of the opposites—he cannot distinguish between a tomb and a womb, or death and birth—Hernández

had not yet achieved such a vision. In the tercets, where tradition-
ally the poet answers the quatrains' questions, he expresses deep
pessimism.

In the first quatrain Hernández describes himself as a man
plunged into such darkness that he cannot know if he is entombed or
about to be born. In either case, he is cut off from the outside world.
The only datum of which he is sure is an elemental physical one: that
his heart—or some throb of life—is beating *against* his skin. It is not
inside him, or at least he cannot sense it there. As a life form, he is
no higher than a bat, dependent on sonic radar. In the second
quatrain he admits that either explanation—womb or tomb—is possible: all he knows is that it is dark, and he is ruled by the dark. Then
he makes a philosophical observation based on the data he assem-
bled: if this dark existence is life, what could one imagine death—
supposedly life's antithesis, a state of infinite loss—to be? And if this
is life and death is the same, then both are odious, and why should
he continue to strive?

The first tercet has several possible interpretations, none of which
excludes the others. The garment to which he is chained may be his
body (which "clothes" his spirit), or it may be a prison "uniform"
(rags, in his case). It may also be inspired, as Guerrero Zamora has
suggested (referring to a passage in "Son of the Light and of the
Shadow," pp. 387–88), by Aleixandre's conception of clothing as
artifice, as the dead weight of civilization which has perverted man's
primitive nature.[19] The first and third interpretations are supported
by a contemporaneous poem, "Man Does Not Rest: Who Rests Is His
Garment," in which the garment is the external, physical side of
man, unrelated to his inner self: "una vida incógnita como un vago
tatuaje / mueve bajo las ropas dejadas un aliento" ("an incognito life
like some vague tattoo / Stirs a breath underneath the abandoned
clothes"). But the second interpretation is possible in the light of the
word "chained," and the contemporaneous "Eternal Shadow," in
which the darkness refers explicitly to the jail's gloom as well as to a
state of mind.

Whatever the garment signifies, the poet is unable to rid himself
of it. The peculiar use of "pursue" with an infinitive complement
lends a quality of nightmare to the whole endeavor. Earlier he was
pursuing an unknown, now he is pursuing his disrobement and his
liberation from another menace, "that which cannot be me," wholly

unspecified and thus more terrifying. This menace makes the gaze "turbulent and distant." Since we have seen these words repeatedly in the last period, we can now identify the nemesis: it is the hatred, the bestial side of man with which Hernández has come into such continual contact during the last years of his life. If he is not freed from this place of inhumanity (represented by its "uniform," i.e., rags) he may soon succumb. The blurring of the distinctions between shadow and light then takes on an ominous significance, not a mandalic one: he may feel himself teetering on the edge of bestiality as well as death.

The second tercet does nothing to alleviate the pessimism generated in the first. Beginning with the disjunctive "but," he immediately suggests that the previous pursuits have come to naught. He is unable to strip himself of the garment, now specified to be a black cloth. It may well be a shroud, still distant, but with him wherever he goes, dogging his shadow, trying to annihilate his shadow (i.e., physical self). The future is uncertain, but at least he will be free of his "garment"—flesh or prison—, for the nothingness which he sees burgeoning is naked.

The vision in this sonnet is unrelievedly bleak, just as it is in "Sepultura de la imaginación" ("Sepulture of the Imagination") and "Flight." But "Man Does Not Rest" and "The Fields Hushed" do not have such a dark tone. Which poems reflected Hernández's final vision? Or did he waver between faith and despair until he died? Given the scanty information we have about his last year, there is no way for us to place these poems in chronological order. Most critics have accepted "Eternal Shadow" as the last poem Hernández wrote, but they have done so for emotional reasons: they want to believe that his last stanza, in a poem detailing the collapse of every hope he ever cherished, would show him unvanquished:

> Soy una abierta ventana que escucha
> por donde va tenebrosa la vida.
> Pero hay un rayo de sol en la lucha
> que siempre deja la sombra vencida.
>
> I am an open window which listens
> To life as it goes tenuously by.
> But there is a ray of sunlight in the struggle
> Which always leaves the shadow defeated.

The final poem we shall analyze is from *Songs and Ballads of Absence*. Slightly longer than those cited in the earlier part of this chapter, it is correspondingly less cryptic. It describes the principal theme of the collection: love's frustration through absence. There are a number of poignant images for separation scattered throughout this book:

> Entre nuestras dos sangres
> hay cárceles con manos. (p. 278)

> Between our two bloods
> There are jails with hands.
> . . .
> Cada vez más ausente,
> como si un tren lejano
> te arrastrara más lejos. (p. 387)
> . . .
> More and more absent,
> As if a distant train
> Were dragging you further away.

> No puedo olvidar
> que no tengo alas,
> que no tengo mar,
> vereda ni nada
> con que irte a besar. (p. 371)

> I cannot forget
> That I have no wings,
> That I have no sea,
> Path or anything
> With which to go to kiss you.
> . . .
> En tu puerta no hay ventana
> por donde poderte hablar.
> Tarde, hermosura lejana
> que nunca podré lograr.
> (*Complete Poetic Works*, p. 424)

> In your door there is no window
> Where I might speak to you.
> Afternoon, distant beauty
> I shall never be able to reach.

None is more poignant than those which constitute this poem:

> El amor ascendía entre nosotros
> como la luna entre las dos palmeras
> que nunca se abrazaron.
>
> El íntimo rumor de los dos cuerpos
> hacia el arrullo un oleaje trajo,
> pero la ronca voz fué atenazada.
> Fueron pétreos los labios.
>
> El ansia de ceñir movió la carne,
> esclareció los huesos inflamados,
> pero los brazos al querer tenderse
> murieron en los brazos.
>
> Pasó el amor, la luna, entre nosotros
> y devoró los cuerpos solitarios.
> Y somos dos fantasmas que se buscan
> y se encuentran lejanos (pp. 390–91)

> Love ascended between us
> Like the moon between the two palms
> Which never embraced.
>
> The intimate murmur of the two bodies
> Was borne toward a lullaby in a surge,
> But the hoarse voice was torn out with pincers,
> The lips were petrified.
>
> The longing to encircle moved the flesh,
> Luminated the inflamed bones,
> But the arms as they tried to reach out
> Died in the arms.
>
> Love, the moon, passed between us
> And devoured the solitary bodies.
> And we are two phantoms who search for each other
> And find ourselves far apart.

In using the image of the two palm trees rooted to their separate
spots on the earth to describe his own separation from Josefina,
Hernández implies that the separation is irremediable, predestined

by a malevolent nature. Indeed, most of the symbols in this poem (and in the others which deal with the theme of absence) are those with which he has previously described the Great Mother, who is nature. The ultimate source of his misery is love, which he twice assimilates to the moon, always a feminine symbol and here clearly malevolent. Not only does it inspire a passion which cannot be consummated, it also devours bodies. The "surge" or rush of waves ("oleaje") which carried the lovers toward satisfaction is also a manifestation of the Great Mother, for she is the primordial sea. This compelling passion (like the sexual passion which obsessed Miguel in his earliest work) is destructive because it is doomed to frustration.

The first stanza sets the tone and introduces the theme of the rest of the poem. It is the only stanza which is not a quatrain, the only one not assonant: graphically and aurally it is dissonant. The use of the imperfect tense with "ascend" tells us that the event went on sometime in the past and may even have continued into the present. The use of the preterite with "embrace," however, dashes such a possibility. Their love was never satisfied.

The second stanza centers around oral communication between the lovers. They drew close to this form of communion, but they were thwarted by a nameless, savage force, grief or anger or separation, which mutilated their voices. The use of "arrullo," which may mean cooing and billing as well as lullaby, leaves in ambiguity the state which they almost achieved. Happy lovers (symbolized by turtledoves), or happy parents, or both? It is probably the latter, for in two other poems (58, "Palomar del arrullo," "Dovecote of the lullaby," and "Song," pp. 421–22) Hernández describes the home with their child therein as a dovecote. (Both Guerrero Zamora, pp. 338–42 and Cano Ballesta, pp. 83–84, have pointed out the fundamental importance of the images of the home, bedroom, and the bed itself in Hernández's last works. Like Josefina's womb, these places represented a refuge from the loveless, violent world outside.) Perhaps it is the child's death which has caused the lovers' alienation:

> Palomar, palomar
> derribado, desierto,
> sin arrullo por nunca jamás. (p. 383)

>Dovecote, dovecote
>Destroyed, deserted,
>Without lullaby forevermore.

Since they cannot communicate, the organs of communication degenerate into uselessness.

The third stanza also deals with thwarted communication, in this case sexual. Their bodies literally burn for each other, but another nameless force frustrates them. Used at various times in the third period to represent affective communication (such as embracing), arms here come to the same fate as the unused lips. They atrophy and die. In both stanzas Hernández's insistence on the physical aspect of the separation is noteworthy. He had not yet begun to retreat from that earthiness which had always characterized him. Within a year, he would have changed.

The final stanza summarizes the previous three. The first verb is in the preterite, as are all the verbs in the poem after that tantalizing "ascendía": their love is consigned to the dead past. The unused bodies, like their lips and arms, are destroyed, devoured by unfulfilled love. The last sentence is the only one in the present tense; it tells us what has become of the lovers: they are no more than phantoms. Yet even disembodied they continue to search for each other; and even as spirits, they are unsuccessful.

Most of the poems in *Songs and Ballads* reflect the despair we see in "Love ascended between us." It is as though Hernández expended—or feigned—all of his optimism in those beautiful letters to Josefina, in which he joked, made plans for the future, lied about his sentence, gave her advice, sent countless messages to Manolo, and dreamed. We find few poetic traces of that buoyancy. Here and there a poem dedicated to Manuel Miguel could elicit a moment of joy, as in the moving "Lullaby of the Onion":

>Tu risa me hace libre,
>me pone alas.
>Soledades me quita,
>cárcel me arranca.
>. . . . .
>Porvenir de mis huesos
>y de mi amor. (pp. 418–19)

Your smile sets me free,
Gives me wings.
It takes my loneliness from me,
Snatches away my jail.
. . . .
Future of my bones
And of my love.

One final poem which we shall consider from the *Songs and Ballads of Absence* offers a sustained note of hope. Its title, "(Antes del odio)" ("[Before Hatred]"), rather belies such hopefulness, for it suggests that hatred is approaching inevitably. In this poem Hernández perceives that love has been the cause of all his vicissitudes. From the destructive sexual passion of the first period to his physically debilitating commitment to the cause of the have-nots in the second, to his imprisonment (which he could have avoided had he fled Spain and his family or had he apostasized) and death, Hernández was a man driven by his passion, which was love.

Beso soy, sombra con sombra.
Beso, dolor con dolor,
por haberme enamorado,
. . . .
Odio, vida: ¡cuánto odio
sólo por amor!
. . . .
Todo lo que significa
golondrinas, ascensión,
claridad, anchura, aire,
decidido espacio, sol,
horizonte aleteante,
sepultado en un rincón.
Espesura, mar, desierto,
sangre, monte rodador,
libertades de mi alma
clamorosas de pasión,
desfilando por mi cuerpo,
donde no se quedan, no,
pero donde se despliegan,
sólo por amor.

Porque dentro de la triste
guirnalda del eslabón,
. . . .

alto, alegre, libre soy.
Alto, alegre, libre, libre,
sólo por amor.

No, no hay cárcel para el hombre.
No podrán atarme, no.
Este mundo de cadenas
me es pequeño y exterior.
¿Quién encierra una sonrisa?
¿Quién amuralla una voz?
. . . .

A lo lejos tú, sintiendo
en tus brazos mi prisión,
en tus brazos donde late
la libertad de los dos.
Libre soy, siénteme libre.
Sólo por amor. (pp. 403–05)[20]

I am a kiss, shadow with shadow.
Kiss, sorrow with sorrow,
For having fallen in love,
. . . .
Hatred, life: so much hatred
Just for love!
. . . .

All that is signified by
Swallows, ascension,
Clarity, breadth, air,
Decided space, sun,
Fluttering horizon,
Interred in a corner.
Thickness, sea, desert,
Blood, rolling mountain,
Liberties of my soul
Clamorous from passion,
Parading through my body
Where they do not stay, no,
But where they are deployed,
Just for love.

Because within the sad
Garland of iron,
. . . .
Noble, happy, and free am I.

Noble, happy, free, free,
Just because of love.

No, there is no prison for man.
They cannot bind me, no.
This world of chains
Is small and beneath me.
Who locks up a smile?
Who walls in a voice?
. . . .
Far in the distance you, feeling
My prison in your arms,
In your arms where
The liberty of both beats.
I am free, feel me to be free.
Just for love.

CHAPTER 5

Conclusion

I T is difficult to assess the influence Hernández may have had on postwar Spanish poetry. There are practical problems: his work has been censored to one degree or another ever since the war, especially the war poetry, which some critics have nonetheless suggested was seminal in the new wave of social poetry which arose in the 1940's and culminated during the 1950's in such well-known figures as Blas de Otero and Gabriel Celaya. It has been said that much of Hernández's last poetry circulated from hand to hand during the most repressive years of censorship, but because of the continuing surveillance of intellectuals in Spain, no one has yet come forth to document these claims, or to specify which poems were in general, if surreptitious, circulation.

And there are other, theoretical, problems which hinder any sort of definitive assessment of Hernández's influence. Too little time has elapsed since his death for a clear perspective on twentieth-century poetry to have been reached. Poets who now seem "major voices" may well be dwarfed by greater geniuses not yet born; movements whose antecedents and influences seem clear may look different fifty years hence. Finally, how can we determine whether Hernández was a brilliant precursor or a voice consciously imitated by the poets who followed him?

With these caveats firmly in mind, we may begin our considera-tion of Hernández's place in postwar Spain. When *The Unending Thunderbolt* was published in January, 1936, it was enthusiastically reviewed by the foremost champion of "pure" poetry in Spain, Juan Ramón Jiménez. He noted its traditional "wrappings" but especially praised the effect of the "rude, tremendous beauty of his deep-rooted heart [which] bursts open the package and overflows, like elemental, naked Nature" (Cano Ballesta, p. 43). In this brief re-view, Jiménez had identified the two aspects of *Thunderbolt* which

174

were to resound in later poets: its mastery of classical form, which the postwar *garcilasistas* among others would strive to equal;[1] and its unabashedly passionate, iconoclastically human content. Bousoño suggests that it was in this ability to reconcile his radically human vision with Spanish poetic tradition both recent (Neruda and Aleixandre) and classical (the Golden Age poets), that Hernández's greatest genius lay: "In this precisely lies his originality, and this is what to a great extent permitted him the possibility of being a guide for younger poets. Because, to my mind, the capacity which a poet has to influence posterity is usually in direct proportion to the amount of tradition which his work, after its novelty, salvages" (*art. cit.*, pp. 33–34). Even in the archtraditional *Expert in Moons* we noted the young poet's considerable originality in choice of topic and in vocabulary. His war poetry was similar to that of his fellow poets, and yet different somehow, as Lechner points out: more committed, more combative, more *humanly* involved. And this fusion between traditional form and original vision certainly continues through the prison poetry, as Díez makes clear. Based then on Bousoño's evaluation of what a poet must have to affect posterity, Hernández's *potential* for influence is excellent.

Returning once again to *Thunderbolt*, which, as we noted in Chapter 2, was not a traditional collection of love poetry inasmuch as the poet and his pain, not the beloved, are the subject of most of the poems, we find another potentially seminal innovation. Hernández has taken the subject of this passion, himself, and turned it into the object of the poem. "The tremendous thing in Miguel Hernández—and what has given rise to the so-called *tremendismo* of our youthful postwar poetry—consists in taking one's own self elementally and universally as the only substantive poetic theme" (Vivanco, p. 542). Hernández always wrote about himself and about the concrete circumstances of his life: if this is *tremendismo*, that peculiarly Spanish, pessimistic, fatalistic form of Existentialism which strove to shock (and awaken) the postwar reader, then Hernández may be called a precursor of the movement. Bousoño writes that Hernández "was ahead of all of the Spanish poets of his time" in the cultivation of "autobiographical poetry," and "since the later aesthetic was for the most part to follow, in different versions, that course, the poet from Orihuela may be considered as one of the masters of the coming generations" (*art. cit.*, p. 33).

We earlier mentioned that Hernández has been called an "Existential" poet, in part because of this selfsame autobiographical character of his work: it is poetry which treats man's factic existence in an equally factic world. Indeed, most of the terms which have been used to describe Hernández's place in twentieth-century Spanish poetry grow out of the confessional nature of his verse. It was "almost a revolution" in Bousoño's words (p. 33): compared to the "two decades of intensive purification and elaboration—or 'renunciation' as Lorca called it"[2] which exemplified the aesthetic of the "pure" poets (Jiménez and the Generation of 1927), Hernández's open declaration of his feelings was revolutionary. It has been called the "rehumanization" of verse, in implicit contrast to the poetry of the preceding generation, widely considered to be "dehumanized" in the sense made famous by Ortega's essay "La deshumanización del arte" ("The Dehumanization of Art"). Still by virtue of its confessional nature, Hernández's work has been credited with encouraging a resurgence of Romanticism, with its unabashed expression of feelings, its pathos, its tone of "pessimism and fatalism."[3] And finally, he has been seen as "one of the first promoters" of the poetic school of realism "which was to impose itself definitively in Spain and in Europe after the terrible shock of the civil and world wars" (Cano Ballesta, p. 256), creating a poetry that dealt openly with man's human, social, and political problems.

Moving beyond *The Unending Thunderbolt,* we find several critics who hold that Hernández's war poetry (in spite of the previously mentioned problems of censorship) has had an impact on the evolution of social or committed poetry, undeniably the most important of the postwar poetic movements. "The existential anguish which oozes from some of the poems of *Hijos de la ira* [Dámaso Alonso's *Sons of Ire,* 1944], albeit rooted in religion, has its source in Hernández as well, or at least if not source, a clear antecedent. All of this means one thing: the poetic position of Hernández turns out to be in reality the great bridge between the thirties and the postwar epoch in Spain."[4] Bousoño mentions the presence of "ethical elements" in Hernández's poetry (what I have called the "inner values"): "in this, too, he was a precursor" (p. 34). In his anthology of Spanish social poetry from 1939–1964, Leopoldo de Luis refrains from commenting on Hernández's possible influence on later poets, but he affirms: "If social poetry in Spain had to be summed up in one single name, because of his authenticity, we would have to limit ourselves without a second thought to writing: Miguel Hernández."[5] There have been published various lists of poets who, it is maintained, show to a greater or lesser degree the influence of Hernández. Bruna Cinti has dedicated a monograph to the documentation of this influence (see Chapter 2, note 19). She traces various of Miguel's key words (bull, blood, earth, mud, womb, love, pain, death, life) which have been incorporated "partially and fragmentarily" into the works of younger poets. While some of her examples clearly show echoes of Hernández, others might well be the result of coincidence (many poets write about "love," "death," "pain," etc.).

Almost all of these lists include the name of Rafael Morales, whose sonnets in *Poemas del toro* (*Poems of the Bull*, 1943) are strikingly similar to Hernández's taurine sonnets. Yet Morales himself has heatedly denied "these phantasmagorical influences," sustaining that he and Hernández have a common source in Quevedo, which explains their similarity.[6] The influence-tracer is brought up short before such an explicit denial: who can presume to know better than Morales what Morales has read and assimilated? None of the other standard entries on these lists of poets influenced by Hernández—Leopoldo de Luis, Vicente Gaos, Eugenio de Nora, Victoriano Crémer, José Luis Hidalgo, Ramón de Garciasol, to name a few—has affirmed or denied this purported influence, so it seems to me that the conscientious critic is (at least temporarily) stymied in his search for resonances of the poet of Orihuela.

Dario Puccini minces no words in dismissing Cano Ballesta's claim that Hernández has been a dominant figure in postwar verse. "I don't believe it," he writes, and quotes Gonzalo Sobejano: "If in the Spain of today there predominates a poetry of realism, Hernández did not contribute to this new turn except indirectly and very faintly, through the 'humanizing' emphasis of a few poets (Victoriano Crémer, Rafael Morales, Eugenio de Nora) who took up where he had left off. In *Veinte años de poesía española 1939–1959* [*Twenty Years of Spanish Poetry*, Barcelona, 1960], José M^a. Castellet has shown that the new Spanish lyric is not the result of any decisive previous example, but of a complex of circumstances and tendencies in which, certainly, Miguel Hernández had a meager role . . ." (p. 151).

The answer to the question of how much influence Hernández may have had on succeeding generations probably lies somewhere between Cano's hyperbolic assertions and Puccini's rejection of them. I suspect that several more generations will have to pass before an objective evaluation can be made. And by that time, I am convinced, Miguel Hernández will have assumed the stature of that other great twentieth-century poet who brought such vivid new life to traditional forms, García Lorca.

Notes and References

Preface

1. For a summary of these disputes, see the special issue of *Symposium* (22, No. 2 [Summer 1968]) dedicated to the Generation of 1936; and Víctor G. de la Concha, *La poesía española de posguerra* (Madrid: Prensa Española, 1973), pp. 15–28.
2. *Miguel Hernández: Vida y poesía*, trans. Attilio Dabini (Buenos Aires: Losada, 1970), p. 9.
3. There are two excellent biographies of Hernández. Concha Zardoya's *Miguel Hernández, Vida y obra—Bibliografía—Antología* (New York: Hispanic Institute, 1955) (when I cite this biography I will do so as Zardoya, *Miguel Hernández*) has long been the standard biography, but María de Gracia Ifach's *Miguel Hernández, rayo que no cesa* (Barcelona: Plaza y Janes, 1975) largely supersedes it.
4. Puccini divides Hernández's life and works into four phases. He considers the two years spent in Madrid before the war as a distinct period; I find the majority of the work Hernández did in Madrid to be linked structurally and thematically to his earlier work.

Chapter One

1. Far too many of Hernández's critics consider his major symbols as though they were monolithic or synchronic, when in fact most of them change significantly from period to period. I concur with Puccini, who believes that Hernández must be considered diachronically.
2. I am not convinced by the critical cliché that Hernández was from the beginning imbued with a sense of tragic fatalism. Juan Cano Ballesta (*La poesía de Miguel Hernández*, 2nd ed. [Madrid: Gredos, 1971]), for example, repeatedly mentions Miguel's sense of "fatidic destiny," his "tragical quality" and "prophetic fatalism" (see especially pp. 67–70, 86–94, 146–47, 252–53). "The great existential problem of Miguel Hernández . . . [is] his always tragically threatened life," which is "the directive idea and the principal intuition" in his work (p. 67). Juan Guerrero Zamora (*Miguel Hernán-*

179

dez, poeta [Madrid: El Grifón, 1955]) writes: Miguel "has an unconscious premonition of his own premature death" (p. 377). Manuel Durán (*Symposium*, 22, No. 2 [Summer 1968]) speaks of the many poems which reflect "a premonition of disaster, of imminent death. . . . He has a presentiment that his life will end badly . . ." (p. 134). Concha Zardoya ("El mundo poético de Miguel Hernández," in *Poesía española contemporánea* [Madrid: Guadarrama, 1961], hereafter identified simply as Zardoya with the page citation) sees "presentiments" and "presages of death" (p. 660) in *Thunderbolt;* a "certainty that his star is unlucky" and a "prevision of his bloody fate" (p. 666) in later works.

Such conclusions are critically suspect because they have been arrived at—unavoidably—with hindsight. As Gabriel Berns writes ("Violence and Poetic Expression: A Study of the Poetry of Miguel Hernández," Diss. Ohio State 1968), comparing the mythified and thereby distorted Lorca to Hernández: "the natural, albeit rather acritical, reaction to the mysteriously shrouded aspects of an artist's life and, in particular, his death, is to discover in almost everything which was composed prior to the fatal outcome, a reflection of what was inexorably to come to pass" (p. 5). Moreover, a review of the facts of Hernández's *life* suggests that there are far simpler explanations than psychic precognition of his death for the pessimistic tone of many of his poems.

3. Cf. Timothy Rogers's dissertation, "The Aspects of the Theme of Love in the Poetry of Miguel Hernández" (Indiana University 1971). Rogers considers sexual or emotional desire or love for a woman to be the single most important theme in Hernández's poetry. Our principal difference in interpretation (aside from the fact that I differentiate between the themes of sex and love) is that Rogers apparently does not consider Hernández's love for his fellow man (so important from the war onward) to be an "aspect of the theme of love."

4. Most prominent of the critics whose definition of "archetype" is discrepant with Jung's is, of course, Northrop Frye. His own usage and definitions of the word are so inconsistent (see, for example, *Fables of Identity: Studies in Poetic Mythology* [New York: Harcourt, Brace and World, 1963], pp. 15, 25, 120; and *Anatomy of Criticism: Four Studies* [1957; rpt. New York: Atheneum, 1966], p. 99) as to be valueless in a critical discussion.

5. Cited in Joseph Campbell, *The Hero with A Thousand Faces* (1959; rpt. New York: World, 1969), p. 18, n. 18.

6. *Images and Symbols: Studies in Religious Symbolism,* trans. Philip Mairet (1952; rpt. New York: Sheed and Ward, 1969), p. 159.

7. *The Origins and History of Consciousness,* trans. R. F. C. Hull (1954; rpt. Princeton: Princeton University Press, 1970), p. xvi. Hereafter this book will be referred to as *Origins.*

8. While every man who matures passes under the dominance of the successive archetypes, it is the artist who is best able to externalize this

changing dominance. He does so especially through symbols, through which he is able to express the otherwise unrepresentable unconscious content of the archetypes. See Neumann, *Art and the Creative Unconscious*, trans. Ralph Manheim (Princeton: Princeton University Press, 1959).

Chapter Two

1. Hernández's widow, Josefina Manresa, objects strongly to the unsympathetic picture many critics have painted of her father-in-law. "He was a good man, grave and proper. Everyone in Orihuela called Miguel 'that crazy boy, the poet.' In such an atmosphere, how could his father have been expected to appreciate Miguel's extraordinary talent?" (From an interview with the author in Elche, March 17, 1977.)

2. Zardoya, *Miguel Hernández*, p. 10, n. 15. Sijé drew up Miguel's "literary-psychological radioscopy" on the eve of the poet's trip to Madrid. It gives us a good idea of the literary influences on Miguel up to that time.

Personality	250
Gabriel Miró	100
Spanish poets (Jiménez, Guillén)	60
French poets (Parnassians and Symbolists)	35
Rubén Darío	40
Classical sentiments	10
Regionalism or localism	1

Cited in Vicente Ramos, *Miguel Hernández* (Madrid: Gredos, 1973), pp. 120–21.

3. Luis Felipe Vivanco, *Introducción a la poesía española contemporánea* (Madrid: Guadarrama, 1957), p. 503.

4. Ramos, p. 59. The reader is referred to Ramos's first three chapters (from which my information is principally drawn) for a fuller study of Orihuela, Sijé, and the Orihuelan Generation of 1930.

5. Claude Couffon, *Orihuela y Miguel Hernández*, trans. Alfredo Varela (Buenos Aires: Losada, 1967) p. 34. Ifach, on the other hand, says that Miguel's friends were enthusiastic about his trip and sure that he would succeed (p. 64).

6. Miguel Hernández, *Obras completas (Complete Works)*, ed. Elvio Romero and Andrés Ramón Vázquez (Buenos Aires: Losada, 1960), p. 182. Unless otherwise noted, all textual citations of Hernández's poetry will refer to this book. The *Obra poética completa (Complete Poetic Works)*, ed. Leopoldo de Luis and Jorge Urrutia (Madrid: Zero, 1976) was published after this study was in its final form. It presents many poems (especially from the early period) left out of the *Complete Works*, and offers amended

versions and variations of others. It is not a critical edition, however, for many of the variants are not explained, and some are clearly typographical errors. I shall note any substantiated variations from the *Complete Works* in footnotes.

7. Quoted in Elvio Romero, *Miguel Hernández, destino y poesía* (Buenos Aires: Losada, 1958), p. 75.

8. Twenty-three of these are found in the *Complete Works*, pp. 933–59; one each in the books of Guerrero Zamora, pp. 58–59; Cano Ballesta, pp. 326–27; and Ramos, pp. 132–33. Another, "¿Qué es el poema?" ("What is a Poem?"), found by Leopoldo de Luis, was published in *Papeles de Son Armadans*, 23, No. 69 (December 1961), 339–44. Three more were published and evaluated by Can Ballesta in "La prosa poética de Miguel Hernández," *Papeles de Son Armadans*, 51 (December 1968), 266–76. These three and a fourth also appear in *Poesía y prosa de guerra y otros textos olvidados*, ed. Juan Cano Ballesta and Robert Marrast (Madrid: Editorial Ayuso, 1977), pp. 61–8, where several other short articles (reportorial or critical in nature) from this period have also been reprinted.

9. "Scansione in versi di una prosa di Hernández," *Quaderni Ibero-Americani*, Nos. 35–36 (December 1968), 173–75.

10. Two scenes of another play written in this period, *El torero más valiente (The Bravest Bullfighter)* are reprinted in the *Complete Works*, but they are too fragmentary to merit consideration here. See Ifach, pp. 115–17, for further details about this play.

11. From the earliest times, Spanish poetry has had two styles of verse: the cultivated (or cultured) and the traditional (or popular). The latter, often referred to as *poesía de tipo tradicional* (poetry in the traditional style), is characterized by octosyllabic or shorter lines in assonance, by frequent parallelisms, and repetitions, and by rather enigmatic tone and dramatic subject matter. Cultivated poetry has changed with the prevailing aesthetic, but some of its high points are represented by: (1) Garcilaso de la Vega's (sixteenth-century) introduction into Spanish verse of the Italian hendecasyllable; (2) Luis de Góngora's (seventeenth-century) cultivation of a mannered, conceptist diction which was designed to appeal to the intellect and to the senses; (3) Rubén Darío's (late nineteenth-, early twentieth-century) renovation of Spanish verse (Modernism), both in subject matter (the beautiful, the exotic, and the esoteric replaced the bourgeois sentimentality which had prevailed) and in form (he resurrected old meters, such as the alexandrine line of fourteen syllables, and experimented with new ones of ten, twelve, and sixteen syllables).

12. *Tradición y originalidad*, 3rd ed. (1947; rpt. Buenos Aires: Editorial Sudamericana, 1962), p. 115.

13. Further information on the vocabulary and general characteristics of this early poetry may be found in the concise essays which precede each section of the *Complete Poetic Works*.

14. Cano Ballesta suggests that Hernández was imitating two regional

poets whom he admired, Gabriel y Galán and Vicente Medina, in this use of dialect (pp. 18–19).

15. "Los dialectalismos en la poesía española del Siglo XX," *Revista de Filología Española*, 43 (1960), 72–73.

16. See also Daniel Williams, "The Social Poetry of Miguel Hernández," Diss. Johns Hopkins 1971, pp. 86–93, for further examples of Gongorine influence on the work of this period.

17. This poem is analyzed by Carlos Bousoño, in "La correlación en la poesía española moderna," *Seis calas en la expresión literaria española*, 3rd ed. (Madrid: Gredos, 1963), pp. 265–68. For a more detailed study of these devices, see José María Balcells, "Estructuras correlativas de Miguel Hernández," *Márgenes de la curiosidad* (Málaga: Ediciones Ángel Caffarena, 1974), rpt. in *Miguel Hernández*, ed. María de Gracia Ifach (Madrid: Taurus, 1975), pp. 146–54.

18. Leopoldo de Luis, *art. cit.*, 342.

19. "Influenza di M. Hernández nella lirica spagnola," *Annali di Ca' Foscari*, 7 (1968), 82. Pablo Luis Ávila describes a similar recourse in which certain abstract substantives which denote states of mind are modified by concrete substantives (preceded by a preposition): "Dolor de cuchillada" ("Sorrow of a knife-slashing"), "Gusto a espada" ("The taste of a sword"). The natural essence of the abstract word "is canceled, substituted or accentuated" by this modification. ("Lo redondo y lo punzante en la poesía de Miguel Hernández," *Quaderni Ibero-Americani*, Nos. 35–36 (December 1968), 153.

20. See especially Manuel Durán, "Miguel Hernández, poeta del barro y de la luz," *Symposium*, 22, No. 2 (Summer 1968), 132–34. Vivanco calls Hernández the "corporeal poet" *par excellence*, and speaks of the "plastic force" of his words (pp. 518, 532).

21. The mouth is: a small and bleeding wound; a double branch of purplish coral; a carnation which catches fire in the dawn; a silky and luxuriant strawberry; a ruby split into two, which half opened reveals the whitest (fish) scales poppy; flower; torrid flame; a nest where love sings and dreams; a flaming scrap of cloud; a heart snatched from a cherub; a fresh and red bud on a rosebush; and a dagger.

Comparing this sonnet, published in 1930, with "La boca" ("The Mouth"), written in 1938 and typical of the last period, gives the reader an idea of the remarkable evolution in Hernández's poetry.

22. *Teoría de la expresión poética*, 3rd ed. (Madrid: Gredos, 1962), Chapter VI.

23. Other critics who comment on this theme in Hernández's poetry generally attribute it to his being from the Levant (or more specifically, from Orihuela), with its lush natural beauty. See Cano Ballesta, pp. 108–11; Ramos, Chapter 1 and *passim*; Guerrero Zamora, pp. 67, 244; Puccini, pp. 17–18.

24. Cf. Gabriel Berns's description of "the many images [in *Expert in*

Moons] which have a piercing quality" (p. 67), and Timothy Rogers: "the reality of nature thus becomes transformed in the poet's mind as a universal sex symbol. The sexual phantasizing [about] the observable activities of nature become[s] so predominant that it is at times difficult to distinguish between the levels of reality contained in the poem" (p. 79). See also Ramos, pp. 197–200.

25. Williams (p. 100) and Ángel Rodríguez Segurado (in "Dolor y soledad en la poesía de Miguel Hernández," *Revista de la Universidad de Buenos Aires*, 11, No. 24 [October-December 1952], 575) both make this claim without any substantiation. Judging from his *oeuvre*, I should say that Hernández feared an involuntary loss of self, but only very rarely and momentarily considered suicide.

26. "El hombre, sus obras y su destino en la poesía de Miguel Hernández," *Revista de Occidente*, 139 (1974), 21–22.

27. For a detailed study of these symbols, I refer the reader to Chapter V of my dissertation, "The Works of Miguel Hernández: A Diachronic Analysis," Johns Hopkins 1973.

28. The uroboros (also spelled ouroboros) is a Gnostic and alchemical symbol—a serpent with its tail in its mouth, continually devouring itself and being reborn from itself—which "represents the unity of all things, material and spiritual, which never disappear but perpetually change form in an eternal cycle of destruction and recreation" (*The New Encyclopaedia Britannica* [Chicago: William Benton, 1974], Micropedia VII, 634).

29. Paul Olson, in his *Circle of Paradox: Time and Essence in the Poetry of Juan Ramón Jiménez* (Baltimore: Johns Hopkins University Press, 1967), pp. 164–65, discusses a poem of Juan Ramón's (from *Eternidades* 1916–1917) in which the almond blossom also represents fugacity: "the instant / of the flower of the almond." Hern´andez's use of the symbol may be derivative, for we know that he read and greatly admired Jiménez; or it may be an example of regional symbolism, since the almond is common to Jiménez's Andalusia and Hernández's Murcia.

30. For further examples of this genital poetry, see poems V, X and XI ("Sexo en instante" 1 and 2, "Sex instantaneously"), XII ("Lo abominable," "The Abominable"), XVI and XXXVII of *Expert in Moons;* "Adolescente" ("Adolescent," p. 36), "Niña al final" ("A Girl at Last," p. 38), "The Adolescent," p. 41, "Culebra" ("Snake," pp. 39–40), "Oda—*a la higuera*" ("Ode—to the Fig Tree," pp. 85–86), "Eclogue—*Nudist*," pp. 99–102, "Estío—*robusto*" ("Summer—*and Robust*," pp. 102–05). Other poems with the religious overtones of "First Lamentation" are "Cántico—*corporal*" ("Canticle—*Corporal*," pp. 125–26), "Cuerpo—*y alma*" ("Body—*and Soul*," pp. 127–29).

31. Other poems which describe the sea in similar terms are: "Mar—*profundo y superficial*" ("Sea—*Profound and Superficial*," pp. 163–64); "Casi nada" ("Almost Nothing," pp. 155–56). The influence of Juan Ramón

Jiménez's descriptions of the sea in *Diario de un poeta reciéncasado* (1917) is clear in these poems.

32. See Timothy Rogers for a different approach to this poem, pp. 67–70.

33. "Desdoblamientos y antítesis en la prosa hernandiana," in Ifach, *Miguel Hernández*, p. 319.

34. Alexander A. Parker, *The Allegorical Dramas of Calderón: An Introduction to the Autos sacramentales* (Oxford: Dolphin, 1968), p. 25. This is the classic study of the Calderonian *auto*.

35. Giovanni Maria Bertin, ("Algunos apuntes sobre el auto sacramental de M. H.: 'Quien te ha visto y quien te ve y Sombra de lo que eras,' " *Quaderni Ibero-Americani*, Nos. 35–36 [December 1968], 162) documents the probable echo of two Calderonian *autos*—*La vida es sueño* and *Los encantos de la culpa*—in Hernández's play. Francisco Ruíz Ramón in *Historia del teatro español, Siglo XX*, II (Madrid: Alianza, 1971) on the other hand, judges the play to be "a simple copy" of the form and content of the Calderonian *auto*, its diction "mimetic reproduction—at times recreation—of *culterano* and Conceptist forms of seventeenth-century poetic language" (pp. 310–11). But his criticism is unspecific and undocumented, hence not reliable.

36. Hernández clearly mocks the revolutionary figures in this play; he sees them as opportunists who will parrot whichever doctrine best serves their ends. Jaime Pérez Montaner ("Notas sobre la evolución del teatro de Miguel Hernández," *Revista de Occidente*, 139 [October 1974], rpt. in Ifach, *Miguel Hernández*, pp. 279–87) does not notice this mocking tone, and sees the revolutionary figures as antecedents of Hernández's later committed heroes.

37. *"Perito en lunas," Cuadernos de Ágora*, Nos. 49–50 (November-December 1960), 27.

38. *Algunas notas sobre "El rayo que no cesa" de Miguel Hernández* (Alicante: Publicaciones del Instituto de Estudios Alicantinos, 1972), pp. 14–15.

39. "Lo táurico en la poesía de Miguel Hernández," *Journal of Spanish Studies: Twentieth Century*, 1 (Fall, 1973), 100.

40. Pablo Corbalán, "Los toros de Miguel Hernández," *Informaciones de las Artes y las Letras* (May 14, 1970), rpt. in Ifach, *Miguel Hernández*, pp. 175–80, is the best study to date of the bull in Hernández's poetry.

41. This is a theme to which I shall return frequently. Cf. José Valverde, "Temática y circunstancia vital en Miguel He*rá*ndez," in Ifach, *Miguel Hernández*, pp. 216–28, who also notes this Manichean vision.

42. Aleixandre's influence is more difficult to pinpoint, although it is undeniably present in the brutal images Hernández uses to describe the act of love. Guerrero Zamora sees many points of similarity between the two, but he hedges when it comes to saying whether they are the result of "influence, affinity, or communion" (p. 265).

43. See Wheelwright's *Metaphor and Reality* (1962; rpt. Bloomington: Indiana University Press, 1968), Chapters III and IV, for a fuller discussion of epiphor and diaphor.

44. "Miguel Hernández: poesía y realidad," *Insula*, 20, Nos. 224-25 (July-August 1965), 10.

45. "Miguel y su hado: Canción del esposo soldado," *Cuadernos de Ágora*, Nos. 49-50 (November-December 1960), 29-30. See also Francisco Umbral, "Miguel Hernández, agricultura viva," *Cuadernos Hispanoamericanos*, No. 230 (February 1969), rpt. in Ifach, *Miguel Hernández*, pp. 84-99 for a similar view.

Chapter Three

1. This poem has been analyzed briefly by Vicente Gaos (in his previously cited article), who finds it a typically contradictory mixture of the borrowed and the original; and at more length by Gabriel Berns, pp. 105-09, who sees in it a fusion of the procreative instinct and sexual desire with the prospect of violent death.

2. Josefina Manresa, in an interview with the author in Elche, March 17, 1977.

3. *El compromiso en la poesía española del Siglo XX. Parte primera: De la Generación de 1898 a 1939* (Leiden: Universitaire Pers Leiden, 1968), I, 115.

4. A traditional subgenre in Spanish drama, made especially popular by Lope de Vega's plays in the seventeenth century. As the name implies, these plays are about peasants rather than nobles or courtiers or city life.

5. Lechner considers the problems posed by the fact that the Spanish intellectuals who most strongly sided with and labored for the lower classes were themselves from a much higher class. Did adhesion to the *pueblo* imply renunciation of intellectual privileges? Did the intellectuals have any clear conception of what they meant by *pueblo*? They wanted closer contact between the *pueblo* and themselves, the creative intellectuals. They hoped for a fruitful interchange whereby they could take their artifacts to the *pueblo* and the *pueblo* would somehow inspire them in return. But how could the *pueblo* understand them? (See Lechner, I, 253-54.)

6. Dario Puccini has a detailed analysis of this poem, pp. 95-99.

7. Of 160 poems published in *Hora de España*, he found only six *romances*. Syllabification was as follows: seven heptasyllables, fifty hendecasyllables, twenty-nine alexandrines, and thirty-four combinations of the three (I, 200). Hernández's poetry is 72 percent *arte mayor;* the percentage in *Hora de España* was 70 percent.

8. Dario Puccini, *Le romancero de la résistance espagnole* (Paris: François Maspero, 1967), I, 50.

9. Anne-Marie Couland, "Miguel Hernández: poesía comprometida, combatiente y popular," *Les Langues Néo-Latines*, 67 (1974), 18-54. See

also José Emilio González, "Unas Cuantas Observaciones Sobre *Viento del Pueblo*," and José Manuel Torres Santiago, "Miguel Hernández en Función," both in *Puerto*, 3 (1968).

10. Gabriel Berns sees a continuity between the inherent and "self-contained" violence he judges to be the dominant theme of Hernández's early work and the "outer-directed and even totally exteriorized" violence of the war poetry. "The violence found in *Viento del pueblo* and *El hombre acecha* is not contained within any object or subject, but it is everywhere diffused. . . . [There is] a spreading out of forces which can no longer be held in check. The interior violence has broken loose and the surrealistic imagery which is so prevalent serves to emphasize the absence of a formally ordered universe" (pp. 112–13).

11. The concept of the "Captive" is complex. In fairy tales she is of course the princess whom the prince—having killed the wicked stepmother or broken her spell—can now marry. Psychologically, the "Captive" symbolizes the creative aspect of his unconscious which the Hero has had to suppress for fear of succumbing to the destructive aspect. When he defeats the Great Mother, then, he is able to take a mate and to develop his creative potential as well.

12. Archetypally lions are considered beasts of the sun; they are frequently depicted battling the Great Mother. See Neumann, *The Great Mother*, p. 216.

13. See Lloyd K. Hulse, "La influencia de dos obras de Lope de Vega en *El labrador de más aire*," in Ifach, *Miguel Hernández*, pp. 306–15.

14. The reader is referred to Daniel Williams's study for a summary of the debate between critics on both sides of this question. Williams himself finds Hernández's war poetry to be universal and powerful. Other studies of his war poetry include that of Anne-Marie Couland, who agrees that this committed poetry is universal and evocative; and that of José Valverde, who writes that Hernández's wartime poetry is a worthy part of his production.

Chapter Four

1. Pablo Neruda maintains that it was through the intercession of a Parisian bishop, to whom Neruda had shown a copy of Miguel's *auto sacramental*, that Hernández was freed. Others contend, more convincingly, that his freedom was the result of a government decree which mandated that the authorities carry out the sentences already imposed and free all those who had been arrested but not yet sentenced. His widow says that they freed him believing he was someone else, another Miguel Hernández (the name is rather common) whose offenses were minor (Interview with the author, Elche, March 17, 1977).

2. There has been a heated debate about Miguel's religious beliefs. Since the Republicans were avowedly anticlerical, the Nationalists found it expedient to brand them as revilers of the Faith, enemies of God, etc.

Critics who have wished to make Hernández acceptable to postwar Spain, to Franco's Spain, naturally tend to discount—even to deny—Hernández's Communism, his rejection of the Church, his unyielding commitment to the ideals of the Republic. Guerrero Zamora and Vicente Ramos are the most blatant practitioners of this revisionary history.

3. The one poem omitted from the new collection is "No vale entristecerse" ("It's Not Worth Grieving") in Miguel Hernández, *Antología*, ed. María de Gracia Ifach (Buenos Aires: Losada, 1960), p. 169. The editors of the *Complete Poetic Works*, feeling that some of the "Last Poems" belonged in *The Songs and Ballads of Absence*, have altered somewhat the divisions of the *Complete Works*.

4. Puccini thinks that the notebook of poems which Hernández brought home from his early imprisonment was only a first draft. "This supposition would seem to be corroborated by the signs of incompleteness and 'work in progress' which here and there the *Songs* reveals (some repetitions seem to be variations of the same composition in the rough, to which the poet had not had time to give the final touch, make the definitive choice), as well as by its fragmentary nature. But the existence of a manuscript with this exact title authorizes even more the *almost* inverse supposition: that is, that we are talking about a book with its own, clear reason for existing and a deliberately fragmentary structure, although still susceptible to retouching and correction (thereby the motive for my *almost*)" (p. 118).

5. "La poesía paralelística de Miguel Hernández," *Revista de Occidente*, No. 139 (1974), 39.

6. See William Rose, "Lo popular en la poesía de Miguel Hernández," *Revista Nacional de Cultura* (Caracas), 140–41 (May-August 1960), 186–92.

7. These are: (1) parallelism of contrast, poems 24 and 59; (2) parallelism of inversion, poems 3, 9; (3) parallelism of reversal of the sentence, poem 2; (4) incremental parallelism, poems 32, 38, 49, 69; (5) correlative parallelism, poems 1, 25; (6) double crosswise parallelism, poems 30, 66; (7) parallelism of comparison, poem 16; (8) parallelism of concatenation, 18, 20; (9) total repetition with expressive modification, poems 7, 15, 26, 27; (10) parallelism of a key word, poem 12.

8. Cano Ballesta's interpretation of the roiled water image is similar to mine (see p. 182), but Puccini's differs substantially (pp. 124–25).

9. "El rayo de Miguel," *Sur*, 294 (May-June 1965), 91.

10. Cano Ballesta discusses some aspects of this supposed Existentialism (pp. 68–70). Hernández was not of course consciously an "Existentialist," since the movement did not come into being until after his death. Little purpose would seem to be served by comparing him to the Existentialists (many of whom deny the existence of such a philosophy), unless it is an heuristic one.

11. *Obras completas*, 5th ed. (Madrid: Aguilar, 1969), p. 431

12. Puccini divides this heterogeneous group into three parts. The first, including "Hijo de la luz y de la sombra" ("Son of the Light and of the

Shadow"), "Yo no quiero más luz que tu cuerpo ante el mío" ("I Want No Other Light Than That of Your Body Before Mine"), "El niño de la noche" ("The Child of the Night"), is similar in tone to *Man the Spy* and was probably written contemporaneously. The second, including "The Mouth," "Cantar" ("Song"), and "Nanas de la cebolla" ("Lullaby of the Onion") is like "a continuation, an appendix" (p. 133) to the *Songs and Ballads* and was probably written at the same time. The editors of the *Complete Poetic Works* have in fact incorporated these poems into *Songs and Ballads*. The third is the only group which deserves the name of "Last Poems." It includes "Enmudecido el campo" ("The Fields Hushed . . .", which is, mistakenly I feel, grouped with the pre-imprisonment poems in the *Complete Poetic Works*) "Man Does Not Rest . . .," "I Continue in the Darkness," "Flight," and "Eternal Shadow." See Puccini, pp. 130–41.

13. Of thirty poems, thirteen are exclusively alexandrine lines, two consist of 14-14-14-7-syllable quatrains, three are hendecasyllabic. The *arte menor* is exclusively hepta- or octosyllabic with the exception of the "Lullaby of the Onion" which is a *seguidilla* (7-5-7-5-5) with a *bordón* (7-5).

14. Gustav Siebenmann (*Los estilos poéticos en España desde 1900*, trans. Ángel San Miguel [Madrid: Gredos, 1973]) writes that "the use of the spatial sensation shows itself to be an original recourse, and it is a structural trait characteristic of Hernández. The exaggerated amplification of spatial dimensions is for him an effective defense against the commonplace, against the trivial reaction" (p. 430).

15. See Berns for a substantially different interpretation of this poem, pp. 124–28.

16. The *cásida* or *qásida* was an Arabic love poem in which the man mourned the absence of his beloved, who had left with her family for other parts of the desert.

17. For other opinions about this theme see Timothy Rogers, pp. 200–201 and Vicente Ramos, pp. 238–39.

18. Although unsubstantiated, the emendation of the *Complete Work's loza* (porcelain) by *losa* (gravestone) in the *Complete Poetic Works* seems too reasonable to reject.

19. Aleixandre's influence may also be seen in the opening lines of Hernández's sonnet, which bear a great similarity to several verses of "Que así invade" from Aleixandre's *La destrucción o el amor*, a book which Hernández greatly admired. While it may seem farfetched for a man in such desperate straits as Hernández to be thinking of or echoing another poet's work, there are two factors which make it less unthinkable. Hernández is known to have had a prodigious memory for verse, so he may well have memorized sections of Aleixandre's book. And in that last letter to Carlos Rodríguez Spiteri (January 26, 1942) he had written: "Tell Vicente that I always have him in my world—and in the foreground—" (Guerrero Zamora, p. 169n.).

20. See Carlos Bousoño, "Notas sobre un poema de Miguel: 'Antes del

odio,' " *Cuadernos de Ágora,* Nos, 49–50 (November-December 1960), 31–35, for an excellent analysis of this poem.

Chapter Five

1. Charles D. Ley, *Spanish Poetry Since 1939* (Washington: Catholic University of America Press, 1962), pp. 52–53.

2. Juan Cano Ballesta, "La renovación poética de los años treinta y Miguel Hernández," *Symposium,* 22, No. 2 (Summer 1968), 127.

3. José Luis Cano, *Poesía española contemporánea: Generaciones de posguerra* (Madrid: Guadarrama, 1974), p. 112.

4. Manuel Durán, "Miguel Hernández, poeta del barro y de la luz," *Symposium,* 22, No. 2 (Summer, 1968), 141.

5. *Poesía española contemporánea Antología (1939–1964). Poesía social* (Madrid: Alfaguara, 1965), pp. 45–46.

6. "Réplica y contraréplica," *Índice,* 84 (October 1955), 1–5, 8–9.

Selected Bibliography

The bibliography on Hernández is extensive, but the truly significant studies are relatively few. The most up-to-date and complete bibliography is found in Vicente Ramos, *Miguel Hernández*. Other useful bibliographies appear in Dario Puccini's (annotated) and in Juan Cano Ballesta's books and in *Quaderni Ibero-Americani*, Nos. 35–36 (December 1968).

PRIMARY SOURCES

1. Books of Verse (major editions)
Perito en lunas. Murcia: La Verdad, 1933.
El rayo que no cesa. Madrid: Ed. Héroe, 1936.
Viento del pueblo. Valencia: Ediciones del Socorro Rojo Internacional, 1937.
El rayo que no cesa y otros poemas (1934–1936). 2nd ed. Buenos Aires: Editorial Schapire, 1942.
El rayo que no cesa. 3rd ed. Madrid and Buenos Aires: Espasa–Calpe, 1949.
Obra escogida. Ed. Arturo del Hoyo. Madrid: Aguilar, 1952.
Viento del pueblo. 2nd ed. Buenos Aires: Lautaro, 1956.
Cancionero y romancero de ausencias. Ed. Elvio Romero. Buenos Aires: Lautaro, 1958.
Obras completas. Ed. Elvio Romero and Andrés Ramón Vázquez. Buenos Aires: Losada, 1960.
Cancionero y romancero de ausencias. El hombre acecha. Últimos poemas. Buenos Aires: Losada, 1963.
Antología. Ed. María de Gracia Ifach. Buenos Aires: Losada, 1960.
Poemas. Ed. Josefina Manresa and José Luis Cano. Barcelona: Plaza y Janes, 1964.
Poesía. Havana: Consejo Nacional de Cultura, 1964.
El hombre y su poesía. Ed. Juan Cano Ballesta. Madrid: Cátedra, 1974.
Obra poética completa. Ed. Leopoldo de Luis and Jorge Urrutia. Madrid: Zero, 1976.
Poesía y prosa de guerra. Ed. Juan Cano Ballesta and Robert Marrast. Madrid: Editorial Ayuso, 1977.

2. Narrative Prose and Theater

Quién te ha visto y quién te ve y sombra de lo que eras. Madrid: Cruz y
   Raya, 1934.
El labrador de más aire. Valencia: Ed. Nuestro Pueblo, 1937.
Teatro en la guerra. Valencia: Ed. Nuestro Pueblo, 1937.
Dentro de luz y otras prosas. Ed. María de Gracia Ifach. Madrid: Arión,
   1958.
Los hijos de la piedra. Buenos Aires: Quetzal, 1959.
El labrador de más aire. Madrid: Edicusa, 1968.

SECONDARY SOURCES

1. Books and Dissertations

BALCELLS, JOSÉ MARÍA. *Miguel Hernández, corazón desmesurado.* Barcelona: Dirosa, 1975. General study with little new to add.
BERNS, GABRIEL. "Violence and Poetic Expression: A Study of the Poetry
   of Miguel Hernández." Diss. Ohio State 1968. One of the most percep-
   tive and provocative studies of Hernández.
CANO BALLESTA, JUAN. *La poesía de Miguel Hernández.* 2nd ed. Madrid:
   Gredos, 1971. Stylistic analysis (in the Dámaso Alonso tradition) of
   somewhat uneven quality, but generally quite good. Important biographical data. Reprints (or introduces) various poems not included in
   the *Obras completas.*
COUFFON, CLAUDE. *Orihuela y Miguel Hernández.* Trans. Alfredo Varela.
   Buenos Aires: Losada, 1967. Fine biographical supplement to Zardoya.
   Forty-one previously unpublished poems (of the earliest period) as well
   as letters and documents.
GUERRERO ZAMORA, JUAN. *Miguel Hernández, poeta.* Madrid: El Grifón,
   1955. Important early study of Hernández's life and works.
IFACH, MARÍA DE GRACIA. *Miguel Hernández, rayo que no cesa.* Barcelona: Plaza y Janes, 1975. Superb biography, although somewhat
   lacking in documentation.
————, ed. *Miguel Hernández.* Madrid: Taurus, 1975. An indispensable
   collection of essays on Hernández, some previously unpublished,
   others not readily accessible.
MUÑOZ G., LUIS. *La poesía de Miguel Hernández.* Concepción: University
   de Concepción, 1959. Capable, unexceptionable introduction to Hernández, his life, his major themes, his work.
NICHOLS, GERALDINE C. "The Works of Miguel Hernández: A Diachronic
   Analysis." Diss. Johns Hopkins 1973. Chapter V provides a detailed
   analysis of the continuing symbols in Hernández's work.
PUCCINI, DARIO. *Miguel Hernández: Vida y poesía.* Trans. Attilio Dabini.
   Buenos Aires: Losada, 1967. Excellent study of Hernández and of his
   work. Informative appendix on textual problems and variants.

RAMOS, VICENTE. *Miguel Hernández*. Madrid: Gredos, 1973. Interesting background information about Orihuela and Sijé. The analysis of the poetry is poor.

ROGERS, TIMOTHY J. "The Aspects of the Theme of Love in the Poetry of Miguel Hernández." Diss. Indiana University 1971. Consistent, workmanlike analysis of many important poems.

ROMERO, ELVIO. *Miguel Hernández, destino y poesía*. Buenos Aires: Losada, 1958. Lacking the most elementary documentation, this partisan and "omniscient" biography is of no critical value.

RUÍZ-FUNES FERNÁNDEZ, MANUEL. *Algunas notas sobre "El rayo que no cesa" de Miguel Hernández*. Alicante: Publicaciones del Instituto de Estudios Alicantinos, 1972. Detailed stylistic analysis of *El rayo que no cesa*.

WILLIAMS, DANIEL A. "The Social Poetry of Miguel Hernández." Diss. Johns Hopkins 1971. Only full-length study of the committed poetry. Uneven.

ZARDOYA, CONCHA. *Miguel Hernández, Vida y obra—Bibliografía— Antología*. New York: Hispanic Institute, 1955. The standard biography before the publication of Ifach's book. The analysis of his work is reprinted in her *Poesía española contemporánea*. Madrid: Guadarrama, 1961, pp. 643–715. A rather mechanical study, it is nonetheless useful.

2. Articles and Chapters of Books

ALVAR, MANUEL. "Los dialectalismos en la poesía española del siglo XX." *Refista de Filología Española*, 43 (1960), 55–79. Short but interesting consideration of Hernández's dialecticisms.

BALCELLS, JOSÉ MARÍA. "Estructuras correlativas de Miguel Hernández." *Márgenes de la curiosidad*. Málaga: Ediciones Ángel Caffarena, 1974. Rpt. in Ifach, *Miguel Hernández*. Pp. 146–54. Further study of correlations in the poetry.

BOUSOÑO, CARLOS. "La correlación en la poesía española moderna: en Miguel Hernández." Alonso, Dámaso and Carlos Bousoño. *Seis calas en la expresión literaria española*. 3rd. ed. Madrid: Gredos, 1963. Pp. 265–68. Study (following the norms of the Madrid school of critics) of the correlations in three of Hernández's poems.

CANO BALLESTA, JUAN. "La renovación poética de los años treinta y Miguel Hernández." *Symposium*, 22, No. 2 (Summer 1968), 123–31. Rpt. in Ifach, *Miguel Hernández*. Pp. 130–38. Short study of Miguel in the crucial period 1934–36.

CHEVALLIER, MARIE. "El hombre, sus obras y su destino en la poesía de Miguel Hernández." *Revista de Occidente*, 139 (1974), 20–36. The conclusions of her doctoral thesis (published in two volumes, Université de Lille, 1973). Very interesting.

——. "Miguel Hernández. Formas ajenas y poema personal." *Miguel*

Hernández. Ed. María de Gracia Ifach. Madrid: Taurus, 1975. Pp. 155–63. Good study of the odes to Neruda and to Aleixandre.

CINTI, BRUNA. "Desdoblamientos y antítesis en la prosa hernandiana." *Miguel Hernández.* Ed. María de Gracia Ifach. Madrid: Taurus, 1975. Pp. 316–22. Excellent study of a few prose works.

———. "Influenza di Miguel Hernández nella lirica spagnola." *Annali di Ca' Foscari*, 7 (1968), 71–95. Sees Hernández as a precursor for much postwar poetry. Traces echoes of his vocabulary and syntax in various younger poets.

CORBALÁN, PABLO. "Los toros de Miguel Hernández." *Informaciones de las Artes y las Letras*, 14 May 1970. Rpt. in Ifach, *Miguel Hernández.* Pp. 175–80. Succinct and undramatic study of the bull as it figures in Hernández's poetry.

DÍEZ DEREVENGA, FRANCISCO J. "La poesía paralelística de Miguel Hernández. *Revista de Occidente*, 139 (1974), 37–55. Useful study of the types of parallelisms employed by Hernández in the *Songs and Ballads of Absence*.

DURÁN, MANUEL. "Miguel Hernández, poeta del barro y de la luz." *Symposium*, 22, No. 2 (Summer 1968), 132–43. Hernández as quintessentially of the twentieth century with his existential *angst*, his "haste," and his "ambiguity."

GULLÓN, RICARDO. "El rayo de Miguel." *Sur*, 294 (May-June, 1965), 86–97. Rpt. in Ifach, *Miguel Hernández.* Pp. 26–35. An impressionistic evaluation of the poet.

HERRERO, JAVIER. "Miguel Hernández: sangre y guerra." *Symposium*, 22, No. 2 (Summer 1968), 144–52. Good study of the "myth" of blood in Hernández's work.

HULSE, LLOYD K. "La influencia de dos obras de Lope de Vega en *El labrador de más aire.*" *Miguel Hernández.* Ed. María de Gracia Ifach. Madrid: Taurus, 1975. Pp. 306–15. A workmanlike consideration of Lope de Vega's influence on *The Comeliest Peasant.*

PÉREZ, ARTURO. "Lo taúrico en la poesía de Miguel Hernández." *Journal of Spanish Studies: Twentieth Century*, 1 (1973), 95–103. The taurine symbol as it develops in Hernández's work.

RODRÍGUEZ SEGURADO, ÁNGEL. "Dolor y soledad en la poesía de Miguel Hernández." *Revista de la Universidad de Buenos Aires*, 11, No. 24 (October-December 1960), 571–95.

ROSE, WILLIAM. "Lo popular en la poesía de Miguel Hernández." *Revista Nacional de Cultura*, 140–141 (May-August 1960), 179–92. Traces the echoes of various popular songs in Hernández's poetry.

SÁNCHEZ VIDAL, AGUSTÍN. "Un gongorismo personal (Algunas notas sobre *Perito en lunas*)." *Miguel Hernández.* Ed. María de Gracia Ifach. Madrid: Taurus, 1975. Pp. 184–200. Excellent study of the Neo-Gongorine poetry.

UMBRAL, FRANCISCO. "Miguel Hernández, agricultura viva." *Cuadernos Hispanoaméricanos*, No. 230 (February 1969). Rpt. in Ifach, *Miguel Hernández*. Pp. 84–99. Hernández did not rehumanize so much as he "renaturalized" Spanish poetry.

VALVERDE, JOSÉ. "Temática y circunstancia vital en Miguel Hernández." *Miguel Hernández*. Ed. María de Gracia Ifach. Madrid: Taurus, 1975. Pp. 216–28. Exceptional study of the war poetry. Importance of antitheses in Hernández.

VIVANCO, LUIS FELIPE. "Miguel Hernández bañando su palabra en corazón." *Introducción a la poesía española contemporánea*. Madrid: Ediciones Guadarrama, 1957. Pp. 499–561. Excerpted in Ifach, *Miguel Hernández*. Pp. 118–30. Studies the development of Hernández's style and his relation to Spanish poetic tradition.

3. Special Issues of Journals Dedicated to Hernández

Cuadernos de Ágora, Nos. 49–50 (November–December 1960). Various short but excellent articles, especially those by Gerardo Diego, Vicente Gaos, Carlos Bousoño, and Luis Felipe Vivanco.

Quaderni Ibero-Americani, Nos. 35–36 (December 1968). More fine articles (and an excellent bibliography) by Oreste Macrí, Dario Puccini, Pablo Luis Ávila, Giovanni Maria Bertini, and Bruna Cinti. (See Notes for complete references.)

Puerto, 3 (1968). Articles of passing interest.

The Sixties, 9 (Spring 1967). Translations into English of nine poems and of writings about Hernández by Neruda, Alberti, Lorca, Aleixandre, and Celaya.

4. Translation of Hernández's Work into English

The Sixties (see above).

BALAND, TIMOTHY AND HARDIE ST. MARTIN. *Selected Poems: Miguel Hernández and Blas de Otero*. Boston: Beacon Press, 1972.

5. Books about the Period with Special Relevance to Hernández

CANO, JOSÉ LUIS. *Poesía española contemporánea: Generaciones de posguerra*. Madrid: Ediciones Guadarrama, 1974. Collection of articles (written originally for *Ínsula*) about some of the important poets and trends of the two postwar generations.

CANO BALLESTA, JUAN. *La poesía española entre pureza y revolución (1930–1936)*. Madrid: Gredos, 1972. Excellent study of the literarily turbulent First Republic, when the new wave of "impure" or committed poetry sought to displace the symbolist or "pure" school. Hernández's work mirrors the changing esthetics of the period.

CONCHA, VÍCTOR G. DE LA. *La poesía española de posguerra: Teoría e historia de sus movimientos*. Madrid: Prensa Española, 1973. Fine study of the ten years after the Civil War. Little on Hernández himself; more (*passim*) on his influence on younger poets (especially Rafael Morales).

LECHNER, JAN. *El compromiso en la poesía española del Siglo XX. Parte primera: De la Generación de 1898 a 1939.* 2 vols. Leiden: Universitaire Pers Leiden, 1968. Superb study (Vol. I) and anthology (Vol. II) of the committed poetry in Spain from the Generation of 1898 through the Civil War.

LUIS, LEOPOLDO DE. *Poesía española contemporánea. Antología (1939–1964). Poesía social.* Madrid: Alfaguara, 1965. Finds Hernández the pre-eminent social poet of Spain.

PUCCINI, DARIO. *Le romancero de la résistance espagnole.* Paris: François Maspero, 1967. 2 vols. Brief study and sampling of the war verse; superseded by Lechner. Hernández as precursor of postwar poetic currents.

SIEBENMANN, GUSTAV. *Los estilos poéticos en España desde 1900.* Trans. Ángel San Miguel. Madrid: Gredos, 1973. Studies the evolution of poetic styles in Spain, measuring them against the "modern" European lyric. Considers Hernández's Gongorism, Neo–Popularism, and his role as a precursor to the postwar Neo-Romantics.

Symposium, 22, No. 2 (Summer 1968). The Generation of 1936.

Index

Hernández's works are listed by genre and alphabetized in English under his name; Spanish titles follow in parentheses. Those poems which receive significant treatment in the text will be indexed by title or first line under the name of the collection in which they appear in the *Complete Works*. (Three poems published in the *Complete Poetic Works* are listed under Miscellaneous.)

DATE DUE

GAYLORD			PRINTED IN U.S.A.